ON THINKING THE HUMAN

ON THINKING THE HUMAN

Resolutions of Difficult Notions

Robert W. Jenson

William B. Eerdmans Publishing Company
Grand Rapids, Michigan / Cambridge, U.K.

Wm. B. Eerdmans Publishing Co.
255 Jefferson Ave. S.E., Grand Rapids, Michigan 49503 /
P.O. Box 163, Cambridge CB3 9PU U.K.

Printed in the United States of America

08 07 06 05 04 03 7 6 5 4 3 2 1

Library of Congress Cataloging-in-Publication Data

Jenson, Robert W.
On thinking the human: resolutions of difficult notions / Robert W. Jenson.
p. cm.
Includes bibliographical references and index.
ISBN 0-8028-2114-6 (pbk.)
1. Man (Christian theology) 2. Trinity. I. Title.
BT701.3.J46 2003
233 — dc21
2003049062

www.eerdmans.com

For Wallace Alston

with admiration and gratitude

Contents

Preface

| | |

This small book must be introduced by yet another invocation of an old saw. Γνῶθι σεαυτόν, the West's founding thinkers notoriously laid down: know first yourself. We have been obedient to the mandate; the long argument of Western thinking has circled endlessly around it. Our philosophy and theology and their legitimate and illegitimate offspring have labored obsessively to improve and extend knowledge of ourselves, of what we may call "the human" and of ourselves as human.

But one cannot successfully think *about* what one cannot quite think at all. Our anthropological endeavors are at once impelled and checked by an epistemic quirk or set of quirks: notions we need to use and do use when we talk about ourselves as human resist being thought. This book results from repeated experience of how hard it is simply to get certain notions into our heads, that nevertheless we do and must use if we are to interpret our humanity to ourselves.

The chapter on death was written first and so came to be a sort of paradigm for the rest of the book, which is why it has its perhaps surprising position as the first chapter — readers should in any case be aware that the order of chapters has only a little systematic significance. As a theologian and preacher, I have of course often had to speak and write about death, but with each year have been more struck by the extraordinary difficulty we have in *thinking* death and not just putting words on paper or into the air. For a merely preliminary evocation of the difficulty, I simply invite the reader to try to think his or her own death, and observe what happens. It is all very well to utter the sentence, "I will die." But when we try to pair this sentence with what Hegel called a *Vorstellung,* a mental representation of the concept ". . . will die," to bring the concept into the actual flow of living reflection, we find that what we produce is always in fact the representation of a continued consciousness of some however unpleasing sort, that is, of not being quite dead. Asked to give a lecture to graduate students of religion at the University of Virginia, I thought of offering some reflections on this difficulty, and proposed a way to think death that relies on invoking the reality of the biblical God.

When then Austin Theological Seminary invited me to give the three Currie Lectures for 2001, and I had to decide what I might offer, it occurred to me that I was already on my way. So for the scholars in Austin I brought an improved version — I hope it was improved — of my attempt to think death, and added similar proposals about the likewise problematic notions of consciousness and freedom. It was clear to me in advance that the new essays should continue the course of the essay on death, arguing that only by reference to the specifically triune God is it possible to make these anthropological notions work well in thought. The rhythmic structure that has resulted may inflict a certain exasperation on some readers, particularly as the number of chapters increases past the three made for Austin: they may come to say, at about the two-thirds point of each chapter, "Here we go with the Trinity again!" I can only say, "Well — Yes."

The chapters on reality, wickedness, and love were written after the Currie Lectures, to make the present book. The chapter on love also was given as a lecture, to participants in the Center of Theological Inquiry's "Pastor-Theologian" program. The chapter on wickedness was begun shortly after September 11, 2001, and has not been tested as a lecture. Nor has that on reality, conceived after seeing the film whose description runs through the chapter.

Some may wonder why there are not other chapters, perhaps on reason or hope or embodiment. It is anyway obvious that the book presents nothing like a systematic theological anthropology, though neither is it merely an after-the-fact assemblage of occasional essays. I limited myself to those anthropological notions that do not merely pose certain problems but that are themselves hard to think, and omitted one or two possibilities of that sort also, because I found nothing material to say beyond what I have elsewhere written. If there is a principle of order beyond the paradigmatic location of death, that principle is perhaps more rhetorical than conceptual. The book is thus less dialectically ingenious than I might have wished, but that is life, or anyway human (!) life.

This preface is perhaps also the place to warn of another aspect of this book, which may surprise readers who know my other more recent writing. I will be much more involved with those we call "philosophers" than such readers may expect. Somehow it just worked out that way this time: I will be arguing with Hegel — especially, for some reason, Hegel — and Heidegger and Descartes and Aristotle and their like in most of the following chapters — though Augustine, Aquinas, Luther, Edwards, and certain bewildered Lutherans will also appear.

Here I wish to assure readers that, however remote from the gospel or Scripture a stretch of this book's reflection may seem, it is indeed the Christian faith that steers it, and if in any chapter they perservere, they will soon come to where that is more apparent. I share Karl Barth's view of philosophy — which is not the view that English or American readers are most likely to attribute to him — that those we call "philosophers" are in fact theologians of some religion or other,[1] whom Christian theologians should therefore engage directly as fellows in a common cognitive enterprise, even though some are handicapped by ignorance or rejection of the Christ.

Finally, I should acknowledge my most immediate debts. The

1. We take the word from certain Greek thinkers' own word for their activity, which activity itself was quite straightforwardly what we would call the "theology" of Parmenidean-Homeric religion.

time at Austin Theological Seminary was good, and the seminary provided an excellent audience. The Currie adult class at Highland Park Presbyterian Church in Dallas, which funds the lectures, does thereby a very good work, and Blanche Jenson and I enjoyed being with its members for a time after the lectures. My work at the Center of Theological Inquiry, the structure of which allows me to do such things as writing this book, and the primary content of which is extended converse with the world's theologians, has been called by envious colleagues "the best job in the world for someone like us." And conversation with Blanche Jenson has as always guided every step of the way, particularly the choice of every "notion" but the first.

Thinking Death

| | |

I

A theologian must of course sooner and later have something to say about death, and so I have been compelled to invoke the fact of death in many verbal and written contexts. And the more I have pondered the fact of death, the more metaphysically central it has seemed to me *and* the more resistant to thought it has seemed. What this chapter will do is display what I find puzzling about death, and try to bring my worryings of the matter under some discipline.

Let me put the puzzlement the way I first formulated it, which was in Hegel's jargon: the thought of death seems to be a *Begriff* for which no *Vorstellung* is available. That is, translating from the Hegelian as best as may be, the thought of death seems to be a concept to which no representation can be fitted to make it actually function in human — as against some versions of divine — thinking, no maieutic mental picture shaped to bring the concept into the flow of lived reflection.[1]

"I will die" and "Jones will die" are surely properly formed propositions, so that ". . . will die" must be a properly formed concept. Yet

1. It may be noted that I am — if any kind of Hegelian — a "right-wing" one, in that in my judgment the attainment of a *Begriff* does not leave the *Vorstellung* behind, indeed the *Begriff* does not function in actual thought without its *Vorstellung*.

with the first of those propositions no representation can be paired — or at least that is the way the matter first presents itself. The only images I seem able to summon to accompany the proposition "I will die" are in fact of some continuation of consciousness *in* death, which of course is to say that they are not images of death at all but of a mode of life, however unsatisfactory.

The late-modern doctrine is that someone's death is simply the end of that someone. That is where our reflections too must start, both because we are ineluctably late-modern and because that or something close to it is where the Bible also starts. The Bible does not remain with its starting point, though it never repudiates it. That must be the pattern of our reflections also.

The sheer end of someone is easy to think in the third person: first there is Jones and then there is only an erstwhile organism, a corpse, which is not Jones. The corpse provides the *Vorstellung:* to envision Jones dead I need only view or imagine the corpse. But in the first person — or indeed sometimes in the second — the first "only" makes a twist. From my point of view, my corpse is not, as in the third person, the fact of the person's — my — non-existence. What for me would be the fact of my non-existence would be the absence of my consciousness. But it is precisely the termination of my consciousness that seems impossible to think. The sophisticated and unsophisticated images we summon when we talk in the first person about death, without supposing immortality, all fail. Entry into a void, total darkness, absence of my self, the supervention of unconsciousness, what one might call absolute sleep, all are of course modes of consciousness, which is what is supposed not to be there.

Indeed it is a point on which the religions more or less agree, that consciousness *cannot* simply be terminated — even though according to some religions it will cease to be individual[2] in those who eventually attain blessedness. We sometimes talk about finding out, when we die, whether this general religious conviction is true. But of course if there is no immortality of any sort, I will *not* find that out,

2. Whatever that may mean.

since there will be no I to make the discovery. If death is indeed a "bourne from which no traveler returns" then it is even more problematic than that; there is no way to enter it either, for by what would be entering it I cease to enter things.

Thus the insight that has held me in fascination since it became fully clear to me is this: the cessation of my consciousness is for me the same as there not being and there never having been and there not going to be anything at all. The actual vanishing of my consciousness is not darkness or unconsciousness; it is not even a void; it is that there is nothing — also not nothingness — and never was anything and never will be anything.

Next we must drop even the "for me," just because it *is* "me" whose non-being I am trying to think — and it must be remembered throughout the following that it is death in the first person we are worrying. The cessation of my consciousness, if it happens, is the retroactive vanishing of being, the sheer occurrence of non-being. And this cannot be thought as being's vanishing merely *for* my consciousness, this not being extant to provide such a reference point. The non-being that occurs at my death cannot in fact be put in perspective; it cannot be made relative to anything, for that anything would have to be my consciousness, which is not. And *that* is: the thought of the ending of my consciousness cannot finally be distinguished from the thought of there just not being or ever having been or ever going to be anything at all, with no "for me" tacked on. It could be so distinguished only by providing it with an image of possible experience, a *Vorstellung,* which is just what the nature of the case seems to make unavailable.

Here is one root of the temptation to idealism. If the non-being of my consciousness is not distinguishable from non-being as such, then perhaps being-for-consciousness is not distinguishable from being as such. I say "temptation" because for Christian or Jewish theology that is what idealism is. Yet as one will not understand Paul until one has understood why he had no direct answer to the question "Shall we then sin that grace may abound?" so perhaps — at least in the West — properly Christian metaphysics and therein a proper interpretation of death can only be conducted while being tempted to idealism.

Within the religions, the impossibility of thinking my consciousness' cessation is not necessarily a comfort. Most religions posit something that can be called, in the wretched phrase, an "afterlife," but some religions have been appalled by the vision and have seen salvation precisely in rescue from afterlife.[3] Since the cessation of consciousness is unthinkable, these religions suppose that the rescue can only be accomplished by millennially arduous training in thinking the unthinkable, in thinking — to adduce the cliché-ed Zen instances — the sound of one hand clapping or the number of a heap.

II

Until ancient Israel's faith became fully eschatological and so opened the hope for resurrection — which is something different than an afterlife — the fact of death was for her, as Gerhard von Rad notoriously remarked, a "strange theological lacuna,"[4] and one that she seems deliberately to have maintained. Sometimes Israel said explicitly that the dead have nothing further to do with God,[5] which to be consistent with her doctrine of creation should have meant that the dead simply are not; and for much of her history that was, if I may put it so, what she *tried* to think. But not even Israel could quite achieve the thought; thus she prohibited necromancy but did not think it impossible. Here archaic Israel's position was much like that of archaic Greece; Samuel called back from the dead[6] was remarkably like Achilles called back from the dead, and about as cheerful.

3. My own first metaphysical thought came, as a child, while listening to the preacher speak of eternity. I thought about heaven, as pleasure going on and on and on and on and . . . , and then about hell as pain going on and on and on and . . . , and concluded there was no real difference between them.

4. *Theologie des alten Testaments,* vol. 2 (Munich: Kaiser, 1965), pp. 371-72.

5. E.g., Psalm 88.

6. 1 Samuel 28:15-19.

Israel's unwillingness to deal with the dead as fellow creatures — even while not being able to deny their reality — is not to be understood simply as a "primitive" stage in her religious development. There is of course a conventional social-theoretical explanation: the continuance of the nation provided Israelites with sufficient survival beyond individual death so long as Israelites' self-awareness was dominated by the individual's identity with the nation, and so long as the nation's own survival could be relied upon. And this explanation is no doubt true in its general way. But such generalities are true of any actual people only in the particular people's own way; and so in Israel they are true only in the way of her faith in creation and in the way of the eschatological self-understanding given already with the call of Abraham.

The Bible displays a fairly comprehensive unpacking of what it means when it says that God "creates" what is not himself, instead of, say, making it or birthing it. To create is not to produce a thing, not even a big and beautiful and wonderful thing like a cosmos. It is rather to initiate, sustain, and fulfill a history.[7] Now a history is "a" history only in that it has an end. Creation is a single something, "the" creation, and thereby is an other than God and so is creation at all, only in that this history will come to some conclusion beyond which it does not simply continue; this is one of the chief theologoumena worked out in the later religious history of Israel. And the same must be true of individual creatures. Since I am a history, I do not exist as a specific and singular something except as I will come to an actual end, an end that is not finessed. As a creature, I am only in that I will not be.[8]

The exilic prophets called Israel to a future not to be accommodated within the way things go now. A chief feature of that future is that in it all diachronic Israel may live again. Precisely so, until then Israel's faith had to consider the dead as simply finished. For before

7. Perhaps I may be forgiven for referencing this with my own work. *Systematic Theology* (New York: Oxford University Press, 1997-1999), vol. 2, pp. 1-52.

8. This character of finitude is the opening for nihilism, for the itself finally unthinkable doctrine that the being of beings is their non-being.

any living creature is called into life, it simply is not; and when God ceases to call, it again simply is not. If it just sneaks past its own end and continues on, in however shadowy a manner, it never was a creature to begin with.

But now we are back with that unthinkable thought of mere termination, with that *Begriff* without a *Vorstellung.* Or are we now at the beginning of a way on which I can actually think the identity of my death with the creation's non-being? Without thinking the identity of being and consciousness, i.e., without falling to idealism? And without thinking the ultimacy of nothing, i.e., without falling into nihilism? And so perhaps think also what it is to die? And perhaps even why resurrection is not illusion? But here we must endure an excursus.

III

At the juncture of idealism and nihilism stands the twentieth century's greatest and most sinister philosopher, Martin Heidegger,[9] preoccupied precisely with death. It will be profitable to spend a few paragraphs with him, though only a few. The early work that made Heidegger famous, *Sein und Zeit,* is an extended effort to interpret death's peculiarity as itself our salvation.

I must of course summarize Heidegger brutally — which may not be a disadvantage since he is perhaps more intelligible in summary than in full text. My death, according to Heidegger, is the one possibility that I cannot actualize, that I cannot transform into an item of the world, for to actualize it I must cease to be and so cease to inhabit a world. Which is to say, my death is the one possibility I cannot strip of its character as possibility.[10] If, e.g., going to China is a possibility for me, when I get there it is a possibility no longer. Not so with death. So

9. That the century's greatest philosopher is also its most sinister is certainly some sort of comment about our place in history.

10. Martin Heidegger, *Sein und Zeit* (Tübingen: Max Niemeyer, 1953, original publication as series, 1926), pp. 252-66.

far, Heidegger's analysis presents an ontological version of the same twist we have been evoking as a matter of epistemology.

But Heidegger construes this analysis as itself, in *existentiell* translation — that is, as preaching — a message of salvation. Since my death is only possibility, then if I live by explicitly facing and moving toward it, if I "undertake" my death as "mine own" specific future, my life becomes pure openness to possibility; I am delivered from dependence on any mere given. For Heidegger, fallenness to "what one does,"[11] that is, letting my life be determined by human life insofar as it has already been lived and so is defined in the world, is the equivalent of theology's "sin."[12] It is philosophy's mission to save us from this fallenness, which it does by calling us to live toward death.

It is often said that Heidegger's project in *Sein und Zeit* was the interpretation of finitude and freedom as jointly the specific characters of human existence. He discovers death as the one place where finitude and freedom can cohere, that is to say, where a human can be specifically human. Finite beings are bound by circumstance and so unfree — *unless* my way of being amid the circumstances is precisely that I give up the self determined by them, unless I *intend* the knowledge of death, the knowledge that what can finally and so at any moment be there for me is exactly my non-being.

Does this gospel work? There is of course first the question whether "authentic existence toward death,"[13] sheer possession of my being as possibility and nothing else, is itself a possibility within its own terms, that is, without an intervention of something from outside, of something like grace. The chapter in which Heidegger argues that it is, is in my judgment the weakest in the great work.[14]

11. *"Das Man"* is the subject of *"Aber man tut so was nicht."*

12. Heidegger, *Sein und Zeit,* pp. 126-29.

13. *eigentliches Sein zum Tode.*

14. Heidegger, *Sein und Zeit,* pp. 267-301. Bultmann's theological appropriation of Heidegger begins with the claim that Heidegger's call, "Exist authentically," is a desperate call for us to lift ourselves by our own bootstraps, from which Bultmann proceeds to say that only the contingent summons of the cross enables actual *Sein zum Tode.*

More decisive is the question whether we should want this salvation in the first place — though of course Heidegger would regard that question itself as a prime example of thinking "the way one does," of bondage to *das Man.* Among the great gifts which according to Heidegger lie in being-toward-death, are at least two that Jews and Christians must surely see as in fact two great evils.

The first such blessing is that life-toward-death "isolates *Dasein* for and in itself."[15] Death "reveals that all being-by the things for which we are concerned, and all being-with other persons, fail me when it comes to my ownmost possibility of being."[16] Heidegger indeed rejects modernity's individualism, but only by transfiguring it into something more apocalyptic. Jews and Christians may agree with the apocalypticism, but must regard the heaven that one would in this fashion inhabit by oneself as in fact hell.

Mention of apocalyptic leads to the second and yet more problematic aspect of salvation-according-to-Heidegger. A salvation of course requires a savior or saviors. Heidegger found the needed saviors in a movement whose armed branch wore the death's head as their emblem. And this was no error, labor though apologists may to explain it as one.

Germany's National Socialism indeed lived toward death; it indeed welcomed nothingness. No doubt it did these things far more crudely than Heidegger would have wished, but the popular version of any religion is always crude. The question is whether the religion's teaching authority finds it must repudiate a popular version as actual perversion. This Heidegger did not do. Later, he may or may not have regarded his early support of Nazism as a mistake, but already when he proclaimed that it was the salvation of Germany and so of the West, the movement's character was there to be seen, barbarities and all. The then still future slaughter of the Jews was Nazism's greatest — and indeed unique — crime, but it did not take that to show the movement's infatuation with death. So much and no more

15. . . . *vereinzelt das Dasein auf es selbst.*
16. Heidegger, *Sein und Zeit,* p. 263.

about Heidegger; his fascination is not a good thing to be long exposed to.

IV

It has been an underground intuition of all idealism that not only is the question of being somehow linked with the finitude of consciousness, but that just so both are linked with the reality of God. That intuition is the moment of truth in idealism.

Just *how* evocation of God may enable us to think death, depends, however, on which God we have antecedently in mind. We will here be talking very explicitly and exclusively of the *triune* God, and my discourse from this point on will be very distinctly Christian — though I think a Jewish exegesis would be possible.

Let us remind ourselves of a few basic points of Christian teaching. One among those who have died is the Lord Jesus. Jesus' death, according to the record, was decided between Jesus and the one he called Father. Christian trinitarian doctrine identifies Jesus as precisely *in and by this relation* a second identity of God, that is, one of the three whose mutual life is God.

If such teachings are true, then the ending of Jesus' consciousness and the absolute non-being from which, with him as with us, the ending of consciousness cannot finally be distinguished, themselves belong to his relation to his Father. But that relation is itself the ground of his actuality, indeed it is the very actuality of God. Thus the end of Christ's consciousness and the occurrence of creaturely non-being therein, belong to the very ground of his deity, to the life of God as it is lived between the Father and this Son. And therefore the death of consciousness and the occurrence of creaturely non-being are not opposed to life but instead *belong* to that life by which all life is granted in the first place.

Thus the concept of my death, of the first-person cessation of being, applies first of all in God, and precisely in God as he is life, as he is what happens between the Father and the Son in the Spirit. And so the picture, the *Vorstellung,* to pair with the concept of death can be any and all of the ways in which we image the triune divine life — whether we do so by reverencing an icon, or by doing what I am doing now, writing theologically and analogously of that life, or by teaching a child to enter that life by praying in Jesus' name.

Correctly to deploy the concept of my own death, I must begin with "God the Son died" and continue, "Therefore I can die. Therefore I can in fact enter that bourne from which none return." And the *Vorstellung* that can make an actual thought of this concept is any image of the Son's divine life with the Father, perhaps an icon — painted or sculpted, or with most Western Christians mental — of, e.g., the Son's baptism, or of his crucifixion with the Father looking down.

Just so, to think of death is indeed to think of death transcended — not evaded — of death located in a life beyond it. That initial situation, of having to think death by thinking some mode of life, continues to be the only way death can be thought at all. Yet to think my death as "Because God the Son died, I may die," and fill that thought with prayer or trinitarian speculation or iconic experience does not slip in a covert image of *my* private continuance and so does not involve me in the self-contradiction that first presented itself and by which these reflections were initiated.

It has often been suggested that our immortality is in the mind of God, that although my death is simply my non-existence, this is not a sheer occurrence of non-being because the whole of my experience is preserved in his universal consciousness, because I am remembered by God.[17] Such proposals do not work if we leave the matter where it is usually left, that is, if we presume with modernity that God is a *monadic* consciousness. Merely that I am remembered by you, even if you are God, does not help with the problem that presented itself to us, does not help my effort to think my own death. For me, the cessation of consciousness is exactly the same and remains exactly as unrepresentable whether you remain conscious

17. Some years back, Frank Tipler even proposed a rather bizarre quantum-gravitational version of this.

of me or not; and we have seen that also "for me" must finally be dropped.

But the matter works out very differently if the Christian dogma just adduced is taken into account. It is a point belabored through all the centuries of Christian reflection: my existence as an actual other than God, my existence as "a" creature over against a God who is someone other than me, my existence as an other whose consciousness is just so finite, is enabled only by and within the otherness of the Son from the Father. But the Son's death is integral to this otherness and so to this Sonship, and therefore to the relation within which my distinct being is enabled. And therefore the non-being to which I as creature return at death is integral to that relation within which my distinct being is enabled in the first place. The vanishing of being belongs to that relation between the Son and the Father which is the very *life* that is God, belongs to the Being that grounds all beings. The "mind of God" is the reason and will *lived* between the Son and the Father in the Spirit, and to be remembered *there* is to live.

It may perhaps a little help understanding, if we recur to the analogy just used, of the created second-person. There is after all someone who sees me whole, and that is any of you. For to you I am an object, that is, you can and in some circumstances must deal with me as if I were an already known thing, and that is, as if I were dead. But you know the object I am as a presumed consciousness; I am for you a person-type object. Thus you, who know me as if I were dead, nevertheless can address me out of that very apprehension. And in hearkening and responding to that address, I too have myself as my object, that is, have my dead self as the content of consciousness.

With these reflections we may seem to have undone my contention: we may seem to have found a way to think my death without invoking God. But of course this does not quite work. In the dialectic just described, you and I remain each partly aloof from the relation between us. Thus your consciousness of my dead self can indeed be communicated to me, but this consciousness that you enable in me cannot be wholly identical with my consciousness of my self, and so is not truly a consciousness of myself as dead.

But in God, according to standard trinitarian thinking, the persons Father, Son, and Spirit *are* identical with the relations between them; none of the three has any position aloof from his self-giving to or through the others. The Father knows the Son's death as God's own, and so as his own, suffered in the person of the Son. The Son knows the Father's continuing consciousness of his dead self as God's own, and so as his own consciousness of his dead self, active in the person of the Father.

Here we must again take a step taken before: my being is participation in this triune Being. Thus the cessation of my being for my consciousness is participation in a mutual consciousness in which cessation and being each constitute the other. And that is a thought which, however difficult, can be entertained.

Or let me come at the whole matter from a slightly different angle, perhaps more transparent. To speak simply of Jesus the individual as by himself the second identity of God, is an abstraction. For it belongs to the individuality of this someone not to be without others; the death by which he is a singular history is precisely "for" us. So Augustine spoke of the *totus Christus,* "the whole Christ," meaning Jesus comprehending and then comprehended by those baptized "into him," as the language has it. "It is not I that live, but Christ," said Paul, and his whole theology amounts to saying also "It is not I that die, but Christ." When I attempt to think my own death, the cessation of my consciousness, I abstract from reality if I try to think the cessation of a consciousness transcendentally focused at the back of my individual skull — which of course is what I was doing at the beginning of this essay. What I have to do to think my own death is rather this: I must abandon the first person and instead address the risen Son in the second person, thanking him for dying my death, and then take, perhaps, a crucifix as the *Vorstellung* of the thought. Or perhaps more ecumenically, I take as my *Vorstellung* the Gospel accounts of the time between Good Friday and Easter. Or perhaps better yet, I attend the Good Friday liturgy.

It is illegitimate within Christian theology to think death without thinking resurrection. But to think resurrection, we have first to achieve an actual thought of death. Supposing we have thought death a little, it is thus my final responsibility in this chapter to speak of resurrection — briefly, which is anyway perhaps the best way to do it.

The difference between images of continuance, which betray the thought of death, and the hope for resurrection, lies in the relation of each to personal identity. Notions of immortality locate personal identity in something that does not die, and so betray their purpose, for a creature that does not die has no identity. Hope for resurrection seems at first to pose an insoluble problem: How can the one who ends and the one who — separated by some stretch of time — begins anew be the same? But if we remember which God is in the picture, the problem dissolves. Hope for resurrection appears in the first place only within Jewish and Christian Scripture, and so on the assumption of a particular God. And that God is the one within whose life — here, if you like, we may in fact say, "within whose memory" — the identity completed by my death is not gone because I am dead.

Resurrection does not mean that my life starts up again. It means that the life I have lived is eternally presented and interpreted within the community of God, for whom death is no barrier to life, in whom being concluded is no barrier to conscious participation in love.

At least until the eighth century, those who painted or carved or pieced together images for Christian use, who made icons in the broad sense, refrained notably from two depictions. For one, they would not depict the death of Christ. Crucifixes displayed Christ *before* death: his head is not slumped and his eyes are open; nor is this the triumphant Christ of some Romanesque crucifixes, but simply the man on the cross just before he dies.

And they would not make icons of the resurrection itself, in this following the writers of the Gospels. They depicted instead the women coming with spices, or the bowled-over guards, or the angel, or at most a burst of light from the open tomb.

What the ancient artists of faith did allow themselves was Holy Saturday, the vision of Christ in the realm of death *on his way* to resurrection, rousing the saints of Israel to the same journey. If these images bear a label, it is usually ἡ ἀνάσταισ, but we often know them by another and more strictly accurate label, "the harrowing of Hades."

By various historical accidents, Constantinople's fourteenth-century church of St. Savior in the Fields has been less desecrated by Islamic expropriators than most of the city's great churches. In a side chapel, the east wall of the apse is occupied by such an ἀνάσταισ, the most wonderful I know of. The about-to-rise Christ occupies the center of the space, his foot — in the pattern of Roman imperial triumphs — treading down Satan amid the ruins of Death's gates. His hands grasp Adam and Eve, bringing them from their tombs. And around are gathered David and Solomon, and a retinue of other Old Testament saints. If you wish to contemplate your death, to fit the proposition "I shall die" with its *Vorstellung,* I commend you to the outskirts of Istanbul and this great masterpiece.

The first part of the liturgy of Holy Saturday is — or is supposed to be — celebrated in darkness broken by the light of a candle burning with new fire. The great initial prayer praises both the night and the candle. "This is the night in which, in ancient times, you delivered our forebears, the children of Israel, from the land of Egypt; and led them, dry-shod, through the Red Sea. This is the night in which the darkness of sin has been purged away by the rising brightness. . . . This is the night in which, breaking the chains of death, Christ arises from Hades in triumph. For it would have profited us nothing to be born had we not also been redeemed. . . . O necessary sin of Adam! That is wiped away in the death of Christ. O happy sin! That was worthy to have so great a Redeemer." I have quoted only a small part of the prayer, and the prayer is only part of a ceremony of readings and prayers and purifications *before* the lights are turned up and the symbols of Good Friday removed and the celebration begins, a long immersion in the darkness and the anticipatory light of just before the Resurrection. To think your own death, celebrate the Vigil of Easter. Or of course its archetype, Passover. Or say Kaddish, which notably laments the dead only by way of praise of God.

I will end by noting that if there is an apologetic in what I have said, it is this: I do not believe death can be thought, in the first person, any other way than as Christian theology, or indeed as Christian liturgy and devotion. I think otherwise we must always cheat; we must always produce a concept of death paired with a representation of not-quite death.

Thinking Consciousness

| | |

I

Suppose a robot were constructed that in general behaved intelligently, and when asked "Do you believe in Father, Son, and Holy Spirit?" responded, without explicit antecedent programming, "I believe, and ask God to help my unbelief." Should the church thereupon baptize it?[1] Various puzzlements would bedevil the decision, but among them surely would be uncertainty as to whether or not this confession of faith was done *consciously.* And this itself would be a puzzlement, for how would we find out?

In the first chapter, it was the impossibility of thinking consciousness' termination that launched our reflections. In this chapter, consciousness itself is our problem. The theological importance of being able to think consciousness may not be as immediately apparent as with the thought of death, but it is nevertheless great. To some extent the theological problems about consciousness arise from con-

1. The question is not made up. At the artificial intelligence laboratory of the Massachusetts Institute of Technology, one team is convinced that intelligence of the sort humans have requires more than an ability to reason, and therefore cannot be achieved simply as a computer program, however complex the computer or the program. This lab works to achieve artificial intelligence by building robots with eyes, ears, limbs, etc. And for a time one of that team was a theologian, whose half-quizzical goal was to build a robot she could baptize.

siderations close to those that occupied the previous chapter. My resurrected self and my present self must surely be one consciousness, or it would be hard to see how it was I who was resurrected. But does consciousness need a body? If it does not, why does eternal life need a resurrected body at all? If it does, what about the time between my death and the resurrection, while my body is not?

Pondering consciousness long, we may even wonder: Why am I this one and not that one? And pushing this question hard, we may become entrapped in solipsistic speculations: Perhaps I am in fact the whole.

In a different connection, is consciousness perhaps divine, as we will see that a persistent strain of Western thought has supposed? Am I then divine because I am conscious? Or within yet a different nexus of theology, because Father, Son, and Spirit are three "persons," are they three centers of consciousness?

That there should be such a wealth of problems is again odd, for if anything would seem to be unproblematic in itself, it is consciousness. Indeed, René Descartes notoriously thought he had found in consciousness' sheer undeniable givenness a starting point from which to reconstruct the whole edifice of knowledge, as a fortress newly secure against skepticism. Descartes could not doubt his own consciousness of things — indeed, he rightly noted, doubt itself is a mode of consciousness. He could not doubt the phenomenon he pointed to in Latin with the single word *cogito.*[2] And so far, surely, so good.

But Descartes was right about the sheer givenness of consciousness and not one infinitesimal farther. His mistake was to think that with this phenomenological pointer he had an *argument,* and had es-

2. Note that in English we have to use two or more words, "I think" or "I am aware"; perhaps the single Latin word deceived Descartes. In the following, I will often translate *cogito* with "I am conscious of things," which is better than "mind," whose suggestion of ratiocination restricts *cogito* unduly, or than "consciousness" by itself, which leaves out an important aspect of *cogito,* that it is not empty but is *of* something, even if the something is emptiness, and apart from the question of whether the something otherwise exists.

tablished a fact at the argument's conclusion, a fact that would then be as indubitable as consciousness itself. *Cogito ergo sum,* he argued. "I am conscious of things, therefore I am." If I am conscious, he said, there must be this "I" that is conscious; and thus one fact is established beyond doubt — that I exist. This fact is, moreover and serendipitously, the existence of the very one seeking certainty in general. Thus, starting with the supposedly demonstrated fact of his own apprehending existence, Descartes hoped step by step to attain comprehensive secure knowledge.

But what is immediately given is consciousness as such and nothing more at all. And consciousness simply as such cannot be the premise of an argument.

The phenomenological reflection Descartes initiated has itself undone his supposed argument.[3] For it has eventually made clear that the entity putatively referred to by the "I" in "I am conscious" or similar sentences is *not* itself immediately given. A referent of "I" can, like any other individual thing, appear only as an item *in* consciousness,[4] and an apparent fact of which it is a component can be doubted as well as any other: "Am I really like that?" I may very well ask — and indeed often have.

The premise of an argument cannot be a phenomenon simply as such or a mere linguistic pointer to it; it has to be a sentence mentioning the phenomenon, asserting some putative fact. Thus the actual premise of Descartes's *argument* is not consciousness but the sentence "I am conscious," asserting that this is the case. But while consciousness is ineluctable, the alleged fact stated by this sentence includes the "I" and therefore can be doubted; the premise of Descartes's argument is thus not certain as he thought it was.

The closest approach to a true report of what is immediately given would have to be something like "Consciousness happens." Yet even this suggests too much, in that it is still a proposition and so be-

3. Culminating for our purposes with Jean-Paul Sartre, *The Transcendence of the Ego,* trans. F. Williams and R. Kirkpatrick (New York: Noonday, 1957).

4. The notion of an "immediate self-consciousness" is truly a desperate expedient.

trays the utter simplicity of what is actually immediately given and ineluctable. I will return to that simplicity in a moment.

Turning then to the puzzlements announced, let me state them baldly in advance. There is a logical problem. Our notion of consciousness displays a logical twist that seems to be something like an obverse of the one that provoked the reflections of the previous chapter: in the Hegelian language there used, we might say that the notion of "consciousness" seems to harbor a *Vorstellung* without being a *Begriff,* that we apprehend consciousness and can talk about it metaphorically, but fail to achieve a proper concept.

And there is a theological problem. A simplicity of which we can make no concept looks like a divine rather than a creaturely attribute, for simplicity has ever been taken for a divine attribute, and in most of the theological tradition it is definitive of God to reject capture by concepts. Following exposition of both problems, I will pursue a simultaneous resolution of both. Since one of them is theological, so must the resolution be.

II

First the logical problem. "I am conscious" or "Jones is conscious" are surely usable sentences in many contexts. But ". . . is conscious," that is, the concept that seems to appear in them, is peculiar at best. In certain contexts we do know how to fill the concept to make a usable question or proposition. "Is Jones conscious?" we may be asked, which is a perfectly respectable question, and after waving a hand in front of her eyes and watching her eyeballs, we may be able to respond, "Yes. Jones is conscious," which states an equally respectable proposition. But though we can handle many such particular queries, we seem unable to answer the general question, "What must be so, for us to say '*x* is conscious'?" even though we may have just answered "Is Jones conscious?" by checking to see whether a certain thing was so. Proper concepts do not behave so.

So far as we know, only those entities are conscious that are living organisms, have brains of a certain complexity, and manifest certain behaviors. The problem is, this is only so far as we know; there is nothing about consciousness as immediately presented that requires this restriction.[5] Is an amoeba conscious? A penguin? A dracaena? How would we tell? And what about that robot? How could we decide the question about it — or him, or her?

A disembodied consciousness or oppositely a conscious tree or rock are easily imagined and in the history of religion and philosophy often have been. Nor, in the other direction, are the signs by which we sometimes decide that consciousness occurs dispositive: even with the embodied Jones who follows our hand with her eyes, we may remain doubtful about whether she is "really" conscious, and in conceivable circumstances we might persist in doubt even were Jones to sit up and argue the matter with us. Indeed if we are perversely determined to do so, each of us can consciously doubt that there are any other consciousnesses than ourselves, surrounded by many apparently conscious entities though we may be, and we can do so without the sort of general skepticism that refutes itself. Are *you,* reader, really conscious? How would I know?

Thus it does not seem that we have a concept of consciousness that works as concepts are supposed to, which naturally provokes repeated attempts to achieve one. Current attempts usually take the form of "explanations," that is, of theories aimed at covering the appearances, enabling predictions, and all the rest that theories of natural or historical phenomena are supposed to do. Many such explanations have been offered. It reflects the logical problem here, that the

5. Readers will note that in the following I entirely ignore the alleged problems posed or insights provided by the various recent neurosciences. I do so because for our matter there are no such problems or insights. If some consciousnesses are embodied, mapping of conscious functions onto the body in question is only what one would expect. The ability to do this in no way establishes that there are no disembodied or inorganically embodied consciousnesses, nor does it establish that consciousness is nothing but the mapping or the part of the body mapped, and so leaves our problem exactly where it was.

offerings regularly turn out to be what those unsatisfied by them often call "reductive." That is, they explain consciousness by saying it is "really" something different from what immediately presents itself, for which other thing we do have or justifiably hope shortly to have a theory: consciousness is "really" electro-chemical patternings and events in one of the things of[6] which we are conscious, the brain; or is freedom from control of mental behavior by continuous immediate divine inspiration; or is a certain balanced interaction between differing bodily locations of intelligent behavior; etc.

But despite the popularity of reductive explanations and the eminence of some of their proponents, they are all rather crude category mistakes. Two points will make this clear. First, I can explain a phenomenon by incorporating it into a body of theory that itself does not already mention this phenomenon, only if I already have *some* theory about it, that is, at least some bits of a concept, for only theories can be reduced to or incorporated into other theories. But an initial theory of consciousness is just what we lack here; the lack is the very motive of the attempted reductions. Second, the mere fact that we can imagine a disembodied consciousness shows that what is immediately given — if I may for one last time, the object of our *Vorstellung* — will not be appropriately matched by a concept that simply *by itself* rules out this possibility.

Obviously, I am about to offer a theory of consciousness. But it will not be reductive. It will rather consist of propositions about consciousness within a theoretical discourse that already mentions it — for there in fact is such a discourse, Christian teaching about God and the church — and within which discourse there is therefore conceptuality that can be fitted to it.

Any non-reductive theory of consciousness will in a way seem unsatisfactory, in that it will not "explain" it in the sense of unveiling it as really something else that we think we understand better. But if Descartes is at least so far right, that consciousness is a primary given,

6. It is in this discussion a question by the by, but must not *any* reduction of consciousness to something of which we are conscious be a category mistake?

then there is nothing we know better than consciousness, in terms of which better to understand it. Then the epistemic order has to run the other way; consciousness must be acknowledged one of those things in terms of which we explain other things, in this like time or space or otherness. This does not mean that we cannot attain better understanding of consciousness — as of space or time or otherness — only that reductive explanations must always be misguided. This theory will be theological, which brings us to the second problem with the notion of consciousness.

III

Three things have long been noticed about consciousness, notably and foundationally by Aristotle. First, there does not seem to be anything *to* my consciousness but that of which I am conscious. There is no consciousness that is not consciousness *of*. . . . Second, consciousness seems nevertheless to be active over against its contents. Third, so soon as we ponder the dialectic of these two aspects, consciousness assumes an aura of divinity. I will take these up in that order.

Aristotle's introspective and logical analysis of νοῦς[7] — which is usually translated "mind" or "intellect" but which in his discourse denotes more or less the phenomenon we are considering — produced two sets of phenomenological descriptions. According to the first, νοῦς "is not anything actual until it apprehends,"[8] but when it apprehends something "becomes" what it apprehends, which can be "anything at all."[9] In Aristotle's favorite language of "potentiality" and "actuality," "potentially, νοῦς is . . . everything; actually, it is nothing until it apprehends something."[10] In the abstract, Aristotle's anal-

7. Aristotle distinguishes "mind" from other aspects of what we name consciousness, but for our purposes we may elide this, since he attributes the same passivity to "sensation."

8. *On the Soul,* 429a, 24: . . . οὐθέν ἐστιν ἐνεργείᾳ τῶν ὄντων πρὶν νοεῖν.

9. *On the Soul,* 429b, 6: ἕκαστα γένηται.

10. *On the Soul,* 429b, 30-31.

ysis may seem paradoxical, but we may confirm it by each of us asking, What indeed is there to my consciousness except its contents? We will, I think, be driven to Aristotle's answer: there is no*thing* to consciousness except its contents, and yet consciousness is somehow anterior to its contents.

Of course the terms νοῦς or "consciousness" do not themselves denote the chairs or sensations or whatever of which I am conscious. But if there is nothing to consciousness but its contents, what else is there for "consciousness" to denote? According to Aristotle, it denotes a sheer possibility[11] that belongs to certain individual living entities.

That is, though νοῦς or consciousness is nothing without contents, it is nevertheless not simply *identical with* its contents in that it is a particular possibility of "becoming" those contents, *my* possibility as I am an individual living being with certain potentialities.[12] Pushing into language with which Aristotle would perhaps not have been wholly comfortable, we may say that consciousness, besides being its contents, is a particular *focusing* thereof. Immanuel Kant undoubtedly got it formally right when — in his pompous language — he spoke of a "transcendental unity of apperception," of the structured unity that items in consciousness have with each other simply in that they *are* items in one — someone's — consciousness, a focusing whose point of focus is "transcendental" in that it is never itself such an item. A model[13] of this notion is the focus of perspectival lines in a high-Renaissance painting, which is not itself on the plane of the painting where the painting's world is, but is out in the viewer's space before the canvas.

But what space is it within which the perspectival lines of my consciousness' contents come together? If indeed we may compare the field of my consciousness to a painting's surface, on which the painting's contents are located, in what space is the "viewpoint" lo-

11. *On the Soul,* 429a, 22: ὅτι δυνατόν.
12. E.g., *On the Soul,* 412a.
13. Indeed perhaps its "root" model.

cated? Is the transcendental unity of apperception located somehow at "the back" of my personal existence? Or in front of it somehow? With such questions, we move to Aristotle's other set of descriptions.

Nothing is real, Aristotle taught as a general principle, that is not somehow active, not somehow *being* something. Therefore νοῦς also must somehow have this character: if consciousness were indeed simply *nothing but* pure potentiality, it would not *be* potentiality. Besides νοῦς as so far described, which "becomes everything," there must be νοῦς which is so called "just insofar as it *does* its becoming everything, there must be a certain independent actuality of νοῦς, for which an analogy can be the light that illumines what is seen."[14] And here the matter becomes theological for Aristotle.

For in this phenomenon of "active" consciousness nothing appears which requires that it be attached to a body; rather — as we also earlier noted — its immediate presentation is as something "capable of separation" from matter, conceivable without matter. Therefore, by the lights of Greek reflection, it must be in itself "timeless,"[15] for what intrinsically lacks matter lacks the principle of the changes that time measures. The matter of something is its erstwhile possibility of *becoming* that something,[16] and so is the ground of its changeability. In the case of consciousness, the contents actualized in consciousness change, and since consciousness as potential is nothing but these contents, so does consciousness change; but the action of forming consciousness as this or that, "the knowing and thinking itself," is always identical with itself and seems independent of matter, and so must be ἀπαθές,[17] immune to the changes that time imposes. If from one point of view consciousness is a pure potentiality and so a pure passivity, needing to be acted upon to become anything actual, from this other point of view it is a pure actuality, needing nothing but itself to be itself. But that is to say it is in this aspect relatively eternal,

14. *On the Soul,* 430a, 15: . . . ὁ δὲ τῷ πάντα ποιεῖν, ὡς ἕξις τις, οἷον τὸ φῶς.

15. *On the Soul,* 413b, 26-27.

16. As in the notorious instance of a statue's stone.

17. *On the Soul,* 408b, 24-25: καὶ τὸ νοεῖν δὲ καὶ τὸ θεωρεῖν . . . αὐτὸ δὲ ἀπαθές ἐστιν.

and so θειότερον, comparatively[18] divine.[19] Accordingly, Aristotle taught that if we succeed in actually knowing, we do so only insofar as "something divine" is present in us.[20]

The feeling that "active νοῦς" must be divine has persisted through the whole tradition of Western thinking. In principle, I can be conscious of anything temporal, just because it is temporal. Must not then the point from which I survey all temporal beings, and which never appears among the things surveyed, be itself out of time, and so "eternal"? And so divine? According to Kant, the space in which the perspectival focus of my consciousness' field is located is a "noumenal" space at my metaphysical back. But this is where Kant's God dwells too, and indeed according to Kant from this space I — or rather my transcendental focus — am autonomous as is God, though I can never quite apprehend myself so.

One need not be adept in sophisticated dialectics to follow this religion. Thus a bowdlerized version of Kant's doctrine entered early into American religiosity, most blatantly by way of Emerson and his New England colleagues. With Emerson himself, it quickly escaped the limitations of philosophical analysis and became a mythology apt for popular consumption. To this day, the "little spark of divinity in everyone" is perhaps the one dogma of American popular religiosity.

IV

To the contrary of all such transcendentalizing, it is a nonnegotiable item of Christian understanding: no creature has in itself any spark of divinity; the only divinity is the Creator God, while creatures are creatures all the way down. In usual religion, it is mystical experience which discovers the inward divinity, but when Augustine, in the classically recorded *Christian* mystical exercise, looked within himself to

18. In Greek reflection, both "eternal" and therefore "divine" are adjectives admitting of degrees.

19. *On the Soul,* 408b, 29.

20. *Nicomachean Ethics,* 1177b.

find God, he indeed found God, but intolerably "above" himself,[21] as what would later be called the "wholly other." If active consciousness is a divine element, then by Christian lights it cannot be *my* consciousness that is active for me.

We are at a point where we must lay down some theological rules. If the transcendental focus of my consciousness is indeed a participation in divinity — as indeed it seems that it must be — then I am not myself the space within which this focus is located; it must belong rather to that *in* which I am located. Simply as creatures,[22] we "live and move and have our being" in God, not the other way around. And if the transcendental focus of consciousness is thus indeed "behind" the field of my consciousness, and indeed in some sense a geometric point, it is not therefore *timeless,* since that within which we live and move and have our being is the triune God, who is an eternal *life* and so neither a single point nor merely timeless.

We have begun to talk thematically of God, and as in the previous chapter must talk of the specifically biblical God, the triune God; any other divinity will answer to other questions than those we have to ask. The triune God's consciousness is indeed a focus, but not by reducing to a mere point of timelessness or vanishing to infinity. Rather, God as Father, Son, and Spirit is a *life,* indeed a communal life with history. And by classical doctrine, each of Father, Son, and Spirit is other than the other two just and only as a *relation to* each of the other two.[23] That is to say, each of the triune identities of God's life is precisely a perspective.

Moreover, the Son and the Spirit, again by classical doctrine, "proceed" from the Father, who as the God of Israel is the origin of the saving history of which Father, Son, and Spirit are mutually the carriers. By a necessary extension of classical doctrine, the Son and the Father have their *purpose* by and in the Spirit; there is something

21. *Confessions,* vii,10.

22. That Christ is "in us" is said of believers.

23. Thomas Aquinas, e.g., *Summa theologiae,* 1,29,4.

like a proceeding *to* God as his own and our final goal. Thus the mutual triune life is itself perspectival: it has an end to which all is gathered and a beginning from which all proceeds, and both — again by classic doctrine — are the same God. God's consciousness is focused — to be consciousness at all — in that each of Father, Son, and Spirit has *dramatic location* in a communion with the other two that is itself perspectival.

The following step is then decisive for our present interest: so perfectly does "transcendental unity of apperception" thus fit the triune life, that Christian theology must, I submit, regard it as applying first and foundationally to God rather than to us, not as a description of something God *has* but by another classical rule as one evocation of what God *is* — in this like "love" or "being." If there is other conscious reality than God, this can then only be by participation in the triune life — just as if there is other love or other being or other truth this is by participation in the triune life — and we have already noted how "in" is the right preposition for such participation. In the language of "spaces" we have been using and that seems appropriate to the phenomenon of consciousness, if other focused consciousness than God occurs, it can only be by *inclusion* in the triune structure of God's life.

We may now move on to further characterizations. The perspectivity of the triune God is, first, *narrative;* it is the dramatic coherence of the story Scripture tells of the mutual acts of Father, Son, and Spirit — thus Scripture's own chief word for the unity of God's life is "faithfulness."[24] The Father sends the Son and the Son obeys the Father and the Spirit frees this sending and obeying to be love. Since focused consciousness is either God's or by participation in him, we may conclude that *all* focused consciousness is focused by and as narrative; its location is its location within a story and it is a unity if and because the story is coherent.

Further, the unity of the triune God is a *communal* unity; it is not an abstract simplicity but the mutuality of Father, Son, and Spirit, de-

24. E.g., Isaiah 55:3.

rived from the Father, in the history they actually live.[25] Since focused consciousness is either God's or by participation in him, *all* consciousness has its location in community to which the conscious person belongs, and its unity is constituted in the unity of that community.

Kant used the notion of a transcendental unity of consciousness in radically individualist fashion: the whole rest of the world, other persons included, provide my consciousness with raw data, which are pulled together from an inalienably private focus behind my metaphysical back. But of course there *are* no mere data to be handled in this fashion; the world unified in my consciousness is always already interpreted in the life of some community, first the life of the triune community within which I am created and then the life of the created communities I thereupon inhabit. I *participate* in the unifying of my consciousness, I do not simply *do* it.

I am conscious of things from a perspectival point — and so am conscious at all — because I exist in and by the web of some community or communities. Of the communities in which I live, it is the divine community by which consciousness occurs in the first place. Therefore this location in God is *itself* my "active νοῦς."

In contingent reality, the triune narrative and the triune community are God's history *with* the human community created by the divine community. Our belonging to God's story might not have happened; God could have been Father, Son, and Spirit without us.[26] But as it in fact is, we do belong to the triune life, as those the Son brings with him, because his actual life definitively intends others created and redeemed in him. Thus as it in fact is, created persons have each our perspectival focus in that we are simultaneously located within the triune history and community and within created human history and community.

If this is so, then I can be one consciousness — that is again, I can be conscious at all — only if location within the triune life and

25. Whether this constitutes a "social" doctrine of Trinity is not very important. In any sense I can make of the term, it does not.

26. About what that would be like, we can have and should claim no material knowledge whatever.

location within created human history and community are somehow congruent. In contingent fact, they coincide at one place, that at which is focused the consciousness of the specific man who is the Son. The *Son's* "transcendental unity of apperception" is identically a specific location within the human narrative and community and a specific location within the triune narrative and community. He is a Jew, the child of a woman named Mary with a particular lineage, one of Rome's victims, and so on. And he is the Son and Word of the Father, the recipient and giver of the Spirit, and so on. *And* these are not two locations but only one; by classic doctrine, Jesus the Son is but one "person," one identity.

Why am I this one rather than that one? The answer subverts the question. I *am* in fact that one — or that one is this one — but there are two possible versions of this answer, or rather two answers stemming from the shared insight that my consciousness' single focus is not established in itself. There is the Hindu or Buddhist answer, that ultimately the difference between this one and that one is illusion. And there is the trinitarian answer, that each consciousness is itself and not another precisely as a unique set of relations to all others.

The focusing of other humans' consciousness therefore depends on being communally related to this one human. But that can only mean that the focusing of other humans' consciousness depends on belonging to a community and its history, which are determined and structured by its relation to him. And that means it depends on the *church* — in the sense of the people of God, which did not begin at Pentecost but with God's first call to obedience. To lapse altogether into the Kantian, the church is the "condition of the possibility"[27] of my transcendental unity of apperception.

This claim of course poses two problems. First, I do not belong only to the community of the church, but short of the Kingdom to a multitude of others as well. It is much of what is meant by saying that the Kingdom has not yet come, that the church is one created community among others. Second, what of those who are not in the church?

27. *Bedingung der Möglichkeit.*

The first problem is the more simply dealt with. Short of the Kingdom, the unity of my consciousness, and so my consciousness as such, is indeed easily fractured between the different communities to which I belong. And insofar as the plurality of created community is determined by fallenness, consciousness is actually often fractured: "I am not myself," "I am of two minds on this matter," "I didn't realize what I was doing," and the like, are not metaphorical statements.

As to those who are not in the church, their consciousness too is enabled by the existence of the church. Were there no community in creation that was itself centered around the One in whom divine community and created community have a common nexus, there might well be intelligent animals of our species, but the mystery we are pondering would not occur. And if it follows that the unifying consciousness of those outside the church is always somehow accidental, not only fractured but elusive, indeed inwardly self-destructive, this is after all what we should expect with denizens of a fallen world; in such a world it is the secure occurrence of any good that is remarkable. Rescue from this aspect also of fallenness belongs to the salvation the church is sent to communicate.

V

With each of us the viewpoint from which consciousness stems and at which it focuses is that of one of those for whom the Son died and lives, and then of one who is specifically located among these, who is, e.g., a member of St. Thomas' Church, an employee of IBM, the father of an adopted Rumanian child, and so on. Just so, it is that of one who appears before the Father with the Son and in the Spirit.

So — what is it to be conscious? It is either to be one identity of the living triune God or to be one of the community for which this God makes narratively structured space in his life. That is to say, it is to participate in the life of the people of God, remembering that this participation need not be affirmative or immediate.

This criterion will not decide all cases, but a proper concept need not eliminate all borderline cases, only make them borderline. Is an alien, just encountered on Mars, conscious? There is no test but to preach the gospel, and see if he or she can believe or reject it. If he or she can do neither, we can neither baptize nor mourn, and just this decision determines that he or she is not conscious in Descartes's sense or ours. Again, for other reasons than those relevant to this discussion, we should not baptize our hypothetical robot, even one that on hearing the gospel cries "I believe"; and this judgment is *itself* a judgment that no robot can be conscious.

The theory within which consciousness has here been conceptualized is the doctrine of Trinity and the doctrine of the church, at their intersection. These can provide theory about consciousness because antecedently to the search for a concept of consciousness, they mention consciousness, as our consciousness *of each other.* What needs to be done to attain a concept of consciousness itself, and what I have attempted in this chapter, is to specify the relevant situation of any one of those each-others, by — as it were — reversing the order of derivation and speaking of the whole structure of otherness and mutuality as the possibility of each related focus.

Might theory about some other community also accommodate an interpretation of consciousness? Perhaps. But one may be permitted to doubt that a community abstracted from the triune God can finally sustain full respect for the other, or then that theory fitting such a community can succeed in clarifying the perspectival place of each to the other. This doubt cannot, however, be developed here, and for our purposes need not be. If other intersubjective theories of consciousness are possible, this only shows that Christianity is not the only construal of reality on offer — hardly a novel discovery.

Thinking Freedom

| | |

I

I will not start this chapter in Hegelian. One could, I suppose, say that freedom is a *Begriff* with a *surplus* of *Vorstellungen,* and make some interesting points with that. But continuing to play with Hegel's language would run some risk of becoming merely precious.

That God intends his human creatures to be free is central to the Christian message. In the Old Testament, the great act by which God identifies himself, and by which he constitutes the people of Israel, is an act specifically of liberation, from slavery in Egypt. It would be only a slight exaggeration to say that the whole faith of Israel is contained in the preface to the Ten Commandments: "I am the Lord your God, who brought you out of the land of Egypt, out of the house of bondage" (Exodus 20:2). It is therefore by no misunderstanding whatever, that Israel's Scripture has inspired liberation movements wherever it has been taken.[1] As for the New Testament, the two most explicit theologians among its authors can compress their theologies into, so Paul, "For freedom Christ has set us free . . ."

1. Although when other nations or classes have cast themselves too directly in Israel's role, the result has been disastrous; perhaps the classic case is Boer apartheid theology. Making theology out of "liberation" is in any case tricky, since one people's liberation can be another's bondage.

(Galatians 5:1), and, so John, "[Y]ou will know the truth, and the truth will make you free" (John 8:32).

The church fathers, and particularly the Greek fathers, were thus faithful to Scripture in regarding freedom, from determinisms of any kind and as participation in the utter freedom that is God's life, as the great salvation won by Christ for his people. And while Western and later theologies usually have not quite so strictly identified salvation with freedom, all have praised freedom as a decisive gift of God.

Yet the attempt to *think* human freedom within theology, that is, to relate the proposition "God intends us to be free" to other necessary propositions of the faith, has throughout the church's history produced mostly antinomies and conflicts,[2] even divisions of the church. Would the Council of Trent have seen Luther as an actual heretic, and solidified a still only nascent separation by condemning propositions attributed to him and his followers, if he had not so bluntly denounced "free will"? Would Lutherans and Calvinists have been quite so mutually suspicious for so long, had they not clashed over — of course among other things — predestination?

Nor has the attempt to think freedom within supposedly secular theories of humanity been less frustrated. For one drastic instance only, the great motto of post–civil war America, "It's a free country," means by "freedom" the opposite of what Jefferson evoked as an inalienable right to "liberty," and yet our declension from the one to the other is no mere accident.

II

It will therefore be appropriate to begin by analyzing a historical instance of the attempt to think freedom within theology. There is a depressingly long roster of conflicts and confusions that could serve the purpose, but the prototypical instance and perhaps after all the

2. If this is less true in the East, that is only because their thinkers have so assumed freedom as the great gift that they have made little attempt to *think* it.

most revealing is the labor of the great Augustine himself, first to clarify and vindicate the concept of God's own free grace, over against both Pelagius himself and his "moderate" defenders, and then to show why the resulting doctrine of predestination does not conflict with our freedom, as a chief blessing given by that grace. The following is not intended as yet another critique of Augustine. His analyses in this area are brilliant and his insight into the theological necessities unique. Moreover, I do not think any of his actual propositions are false as stated. Yet at the end we cannot avoid a certain frustration, which may point us to a buried difficulty.

Augustine's fundamental insight, against Pelagians or Arminians (full, semi-, demi-semi-, or whatever) is veridical: theology that makes my conversion, or my subsequent persevering in sanctity or growing in it, dependent on my own decision to seek holiness or on my own sanctified decisions or actions, must "beware, lest . . . the grace of God be thought to be given somehow in accord with our merit, so that grace is no longer understood as grace."[3] There is indeed no escaping the logic: if at any step or stage of spiritual life *my* choice or action determines whether or not I am in fact to be sanctified, then indeed that is what it does, and God's role can only be to confirm my choice. Which is to say, God's grace is not free, and so is neither God nor grace.

Augustine did not cultivate this logic for its own sake, but as a pastor, for the comfort of the bewildered North African believers of his time. They compared themselves to the martyrs and other spiritual heroes of the just previous age of persecution, and had to doubt the worth of their own choices and actions; that is, if Pelagius was right, they had to doubt the possibility of their salvation.

Nevertheless Augustine's teaching was — and is — a hard teaching, and he sometimes seems to want to moderate it — doubtless again for pastoral reasons — by positing differing modes of the relation between God's decisions and ours. Perhaps the most important

3. *De praedestinatione sanctorum,* i,6: "Videte si aliud agitur isto modo, nisi ut gratia Dei secundum merita nostra detur quolibet modo, ac sic gratia iam non sit gratia."

such distinction is this: "That we will the good at all, he works *without* us; but when we thereupon do will the good, and so will it that we do it, then he works *with* us. . . ."[4] Or again he adjusts the puzzle that our doing a good thing is a *gift of God* and that nevertheless God *commands us* to do it, by arguing that it makes sense to say "he gives what he commands" if the *way* he gives is that "he *helps* the one he commands to do what is commanded" (emphases added).[5]

But having spoken of such cooperation between God's will and ours at some stage or stages of spiritual life, Augustine always immediately cuts off any possibility of thinking that our side of the cooperation in fact determines the outcome. Thus, continuing one of the citations above: ". . . nevertheless, without God, whether he is working without us to make us will [the good] or working with us when we will it, we can do no spiritual good."[6] Having offered what seems like a mitigation of his position, Augustine effectively takes back the mitigation, by saying that without God's help the person of good will could do no good at all, that is, would be in exactly the same situation as those who have to be "made" good in the first place.

So in the end the strict logic of grace remains. "Indeed there is always free will in us, but . . . either it is free from righteousness when it serves sin, and then it is evil; or it is free from sin when it serves righteousness, and then it is good."[7] It is the act of God called grace that moves us from the one situation to the other: from service of sin to service of the good and so from freedom from the good to freedom from sin, from being an evil will to being a good one. And this only God can do.[8]

We should now note four remarkable features of the first of the two passages just cited. First, Augustine does indeed assert that we

4. *De gnade et libero arbitrio,* xvii,33: "Ut ergo velimus, sine nobis operatur; cum autem volumus, et sic volumus ut faciamus, nobiscum cooperatur. . . ."

5. *De gnade . . . ,* xv,31.

6. *De gnade . . . ,* xvii,33: ". . . tamen sine illo vel operante ut velimus, vel cooperante cum volumus, ad bona pietatis opera nihil valemus."

7. *De gnade . . . ,* xv,31.

8. E.g., *De gnade . . . ,* xv,31.

have "free will," even as something that is *"in"* us, and does not regard this as incompatible with what follows. Second, definitive for our lives is not freedom as such, but service. Third, freedom itself is always *from* something, from the opposite of what we serve. And fourth, there are only two things we can serve, righteousness or sin.

From the perspective of modernity — and from the perspective of many of Augustine's own contemporaries in the church — it may be hard to see how an agent that either serves good or serves evil, whose freedom is correlative freedom *from* evil or *from* the good, and whose transition from the one condition to the other is entirely determined by another's act, can have "free will" in it. Against such qualms, Augustine simply lays it down: "The human will is not abolished" by grace, but it is "changed from being an evil will to being a good will."[9]

This last passage is again remarkable. Note that in it as in the one earlier cited, "evil" and "good" are adjectives: presumably there is a something to be modified by the characteristics so named, something which itself is identical whether serving evil or good, and must be the "free will" that is not "abolished." But note also that this something-or-other is entirely occult: it never appears in a character of its own, but only as one or the other of two actual willings which are not merely different from but in fact wholly incompatible with each other.

If there is such a hyper-neutral will, a will beyond its own actual character as good or evil, it would appear that the choice *between* being a good will and being an evil one must lie with it, for what else is there for this "will" to will? And does it not then obviously follow, as common sense thought it knew all along, that some serve the good because they have chosen to do so and the rest serve sin because they have made the opposite choice? So that Pelagius wins?

Perhaps to our confusion, Augustine agrees with the second, commonsensical proposition, but denies what would seem to be its

9. *De gnade . . .*, xx,41: ". . . voluntas humana non tollitur, sed ex mala mutatur in bonam. . . ."

ontological condition, stated by the preceding proposition. Contrary to any presumption that "the will" decides between its own two possible orientations, Augustine insists that God alone makes this decision. Some, he says, are elected by God to attain righteousness and some are not, and this settles the matter. Yet nevertheless the first group indeed "believe, because they so choose," and the others "do not believe because they do not so choose."[10]

But how can both be true, that we believe or do not believe "because"[11] we choose to believe or not to believe, and that we believe or do not believe because God chooses us to do the one or the other? Both can be true because, although Augustine of course never puts it in just this way, between God's will and a creature's will there is no zero-sum game, because God's deciding something in the manner of God and my deciding the same thing in the manner of a creature are not on the same plane of being. In a typically lapidary and nearly untranslatable Augustinian dictum: when we do the good, "*both* we do it, *and* God does that we do it."[12]

Human wills, whether those made good by grace or those left in sin, are so utterly "at the disposal" of God, that he "makes them turn" to whatever end he chooses "as he wills and when he wills it."[13] God makes the human will turn, *and* because it is the Creator of the will who does this, the created will authentically turns as what it is, which is to say its turning is willing choice. The will that chooses to be a good will and the will that chooses to be a bad will indeed choose, *and* do the one or the other in accord with God's non-competing choice that they shall do this. The point is simple, decisive, and easy to lose hold of.

10. *De praedestinatione* . . . , vi,12: "Ecce misericordia et iudicium: misericordia in electionem quae consecuta est iustitiam Dei; iudicium vero in caeteros qui excaecati sunt; et tamen illi quia voluerunt, crediderunt; illi quia non voluerunt, non crediderunt."

11. "quia"

12. *De praedestinatione* . . . , xi,22: ". . . et nos ea facimus, et Deus facit ut illa faciamus."

13. *De gnade* . . . , xx,41: ". . . ita esse in Dei potestate, ut eas quo voluerit, quando voluerit, faciat inclinari. . . ."

More of course could be and has been said of Augustine's teaching about grace and free will. But this is probably enough to be going on with. For my part, I think all the above is true. Yet I am unsatisfied, as many have been, not all of them Pelagians or almost-Pelagians.

The notion that once my will is good God does not "make" it do good but "helps"[14] it do so, may be in some sense true, but is frustratingly empty. Given what Augustine says next — that in both cases it is God's action that makes any difference — one must indeed wonder if he accomplishes any more with the distinction than palliate his own uneasiness. We may be puzzled too by freedom's negativity in Augustine's discourse: freedom that is only *from* something does not seem like the "glorious liberty of the children of God." And there is altogether too convenient a cloud of mystery about that free will inside there someplace.

I have a suggestion about the root of the phenomena that provoke our — and perhaps Augustine's — uneasiness: there is in Augustine's discourse, as in the neo-Platonic discourse from which he draws concepts, a hypostatization of will sheerly as such.[15] Augustine does not say we are free, he says "there *is* free will *in* us" (emphases of course added). He distinguishes between willing and so willing that we do what we will, and this distinction is not the commonsensical one between what I will to do but am unable to do and what I will to do and am able to do. Rather, as the one possibility a remarkable willing appears that wills some*thing* that might happen without willing it *to* happen. And then there is that something-or-other in there that is continuous through the transformation from the adjectively bad will to the adjectively good will. This must be a will that wills neither bad nor good, which must surely be a will that does not will.

Finally there is a point we have not yet noted. Although it is Augustine's great and fundamental insight, that God's freedom and ours

14. "adiuvat"

15. For the definitive demolition of this way of conceiving freedom, Jonathan Edwards, *Freedom of the Will.*

do not compete, that God freely chooses that we shall freely choose what he chooses us to choose, Augustine sometimes betrays the presence in his mind of a very different picture, the very one with which we tend wrongly to credit him. Grace, he says, "cannot be repelled by however hard a heart."[16] Here appears the *Vorstellung* — I could not resist just this once — of two causal forces that *could* struggle, of a human will that is the sort of thing that *might* resist God's will, even though it is factually unable successfully to do so.

Since it is a something-one-knows-not-what that Augustine tends to make the object of grace, it can be no surprise that he calls the work of grace itself "occult."[17] But surely one must ask, will not this characterization of grace finally undercut Augustine's whole purpose against the Pelagians? For how am I to put my confidence in grace, if it is totally hidden, so that I must always wonder if it is happening to me? The notorious "practical syllogism,"[18] which finally wrecked classical Calvinism, already offers itself.

III

The way to make Augustine's propositions less puzzling — though perhaps even less acceptable to our self-righteousness — has two steps. The first is to see if we can say materially about freedom what he does without in the process positing an occult entity, "the will," behind our actual willing. To say we are free, must we say we "have" freedom or free will, or that there is free will "in" us? Why not just say "We sometimes choose and act freely" and leave it at that? Do we

16. *De praedestinatione . . .*, viii,13: ". . . a nullo duro corde respuitur."

17. E.g., *De praedestinatione . . . :* "Haec itaque gratia, quae occulte humanis cordibus divina largitate tribuitur. . . ." Here, by the way, is the origin of the split between the actual work of grace and its visible "means" that has plagued the whole history of Western theology.

18. As a way out of this destructive uncertainty, some Calvinist thinkers proposed that we could reason back from observed fruits of the Spirit in ourselves, to the presence of the Spirit in our lives, and so to our being predestined.

really need to posit a non-willing will, to be the continuity between a bad will and a good one? Why not just say the same person used to will sin and now by God's grace wills the good? And that the former situation was bondage and the latter is freedom? I suggest that we will find we do *not* need to posit an entity in ourselves called "the" free will,[19] if we do not start by assuming *we* are the foundationally free ones, but rather start with what after all we are theologically concerned with, the freedom to which God's grace liberates us.

The second step is to remember again that Augustine was a bishop, at an especially difficult time in the life of the North African church. Thus it assuredly was not his task to dampen the wills of his flock. When he said, "Both we do [the good] and God does that we do it," that we indeed *do* it is the outcome of the event. His disciple in even more discouraging times than his own, Prosper of Aquitaine, caught the intent: "[T]he elect receive grace, not to allow them to be idle . . . but to enable them to work well. . . ."[20] Which leads us to a great Augustinian who can perhaps show us what to think next.

IV

In Martin Luther's furious book against Desiderius Erasmus's hyper-Pelagian praise of "free will," he agrees with every commonsensical proposition Erasmus puts forward, while rejecting the theological and ontological doctrines Erasmus thinks these presuppose.[21] Of course, Luther says, it is often true that I did X rather than Y because I chose to. And of course in some contexts I should be rewarded for that, if X is a better thing to do than Y. Of course we do some things

19. Surely in any case a blatant multiplication of entities beyond need.

20. I take the quotation from Peter Brown's wonderful exposition of this point in the epilogue appended to the new edition of his biography of Augustine, *Augustine of Hippo* (London: Faber and Faber, 2000), p. 513.

21. To this, Robert W. Jenson, *Systematic Theology,* vol. 2 (New York: Oxford University Press, 1999), pp. 105-8. The tactic just noted is of course straight Augustine.

willingly and others unwillingly, which is to say we sometimes act freely. Doubtless also, we may then say that humans have a dispositional property[22] of being apt for willing action. And that, Luther argues with remarkably modern-sounding logical tools, is *all* there is to say on the matter.

Luther then comes to what has been his goal all along, praise of a very different freedom, the "royal freedom" to which the Spirit "raptures" believers.[23] Here and here only he allows the vocabulary of "freedom" and "liberty," with which Erasmus had praised a "free will" we just "have." Freedom worthily so called is in Luther's discourse not an individual possession at all; it is something that happens to us, by the provocation of an other; it is a phenomenon of community. When the one who "raptures" us is God, when it is in community with *him* that we are taken out of ourselves, we are free in the only way Luther thinks deserving of the glorious word. And according to Luther it is specifically God the Spirit whose role this is. With these three points we have enough matter for the rest of this chapter.

V

Freedom is not an individual possession, at least not the freedom Scripture praises and bestows, or for that matter the freedom classical Western political theory celebrates. This should perhaps be obvious, but much Western thinking — picking up implications Augustine did not intend — has implicitly denied it, by its posit of "the" free will somehow in each of us individually.

What could freedom be, after all, were I alone in the universe? The "liberty" of the Declaration of Independence is access to the fo-

22. A technical term of both medieval and contemporary philosophy. A pane of glass has the dispositional property of being likely under certain conditions to break; a sufferer from asthma to choke; and the like.

23. *De servo arbitrio* (WA 18: 635): "Nos rapiat in solium suum, rursus per spiritum eius servi et captivi sumus (quae tamen regia libertas est). . . ."

rum in which my community makes joint moral decisions; for himself, Jefferson had in mind the possibility of being elected to Virginia's House of Burgesses[24] and not being ruled by a British Parliament to which he could not be elected. The "freedom" of Paul's letters is of course freedom from the law and from cosmic tyrants, but positively it is mutual sharing in the congregation's spiritual gifts. What could be the content even of saying that I "freely" chose to arise at seven instead of eight this morning, if I had risen to no one's company and to no one's concern with my action?

All I am by myself is someone with the dispositional property of being *apt* for freedom if it comes to me. The actual event occurs only in community. You intrude into my life, as someone different from me, merely thereby bringing *possibility* with you, of being different in future than I am now; it is within this possibility that freedom opens. Should I love this person suddenly there for me? Should I take up the task unexpectedly offered by this comparative stranger? For which of those importunate candidates should I vote? Luther's verb, *rapiare,* which above I cautiously and neologistically translated "to rapture" could more straightforwardly be translated "to rape" as in "the rape of the Sabines," meaning to seize, carry off. Beyond the mere dispositional property of being apt for willing action, freedom itself is something I must be carried off into, by the importunities of community.

Indeed, we can be carried into what Luther is willing to call freedom only by importunities within one particular community, of Father, Son, and Spirit. Since our situation is that we serve either sin or the good, only God, as Augustine insisted, can "rape" us from bondage into freedom; only the community of his life is the context of freedom. If we ask why you and I cannot do this for each other, without dragging God in, the answer in Luther's discourse is plain: because enabling freedom is not a matter of causing but of sharing, and in yourself you no more have freedom to share than I do. Only the

24. Although he followed the ritual of wanting only to retire to a quiet philosophical life.

true God has freedom in himself, for only he is triune, only he is community with himself so as to be free in himself.

Here is a fundamental point. Freedom is first a divine predicate, and indeed a predicate of a specific God only, the triune God of Scripture. This is true even of the discourse of a Jefferson, parasitic as it was on antecedent Christian discourse. Apart from the Spirit, we creatures turn to seek freedom from one another; and when we are disappointed, as always happens, are driven to try to *wrest* freedom from one another and so to a "lust for dominion"[25] over one another. Thus freedom in the communities of this world is in intrinsic self-contradiction and so in permanent crisis. Only the triune God is in himself community, and thus can be indubitably free.

It is a proposition from which Christian theology cannot flinch: all creaturely talk or practice of freedom, wherever found, is neither an achievement nor a project but rather a *longing for someone,* for the God of Israel. All talk and practice of freedom is part of that restlessness with which the human heart is blessed and afflicted, because it is made for God and short of the Kingdom is not yet at home in him.

Which brings us to the Spirit, who is God's freedom in himself for himself. The Spirit is God as his own possibility, as his own beckoning future to which he opens. Within the triune life, it is the special role of the Spirit to be the intruding future into which the love between the Father and the Son opens, as must all love into some future. It is the Spirit's role to liberate the Father to let the Son go, and to liberate the Son from self to give himself back to the Father, so that the life between them can be love.

God shares his freedom with us, in that he creates a human community whose spirit is none other than this same Spirit. Adapting a famous distinction of social theory, we may say that an "association" is also a "community" if it is enlivened by a spirit that is, for good or ill,[26] other and more than the spirits of its members. The particular

25. *Libido dominandi* is a key phrase of Augustine's political theory, to which see Jenson, *Systematic Theology,* vol. 2, pp. 76-85, 204-10.

26. One must make this qualification to allow for mobs and ideologically driven masses. As the Apostle says, there are many spirits abroad in the world.

community we call the church is created in that God "pours out" his own Spirit on Jesus' followers.[27] It is in this community that freedom happens; and it is conversion into the church, enacted in baptism, that rapes us into freedom.

The practice of my freedom is that I am opened to possibility by the utterly various and unpredictable gifts which the Spirit gives other members of the church. Freedom is being able to drink from one cup with the rich and the poor, the healthy and the alarmingly diseased. Freedom is having to forgive and be forgiven. One could go with such predications, but it is perhaps better to remember at this point that freedom, also as invoked by Paul to characterize the Spirit's presence, is a *political* concept, even as the Fulfillment is conceived in Scripture as a polity, as a Kingdom or City or People.

The final propositions of this chapter must be: first, that the church is that polity in which freedom is native; and second, that the freedom spoken of and practiced by the polities of this world is but aspiration to the church's freedom. That the church is far from perfect, and imperfect especially in her politics, we know all too well. But short of the End, perfection is never the point. In the church, even at its most appropriately or inappropriately hierarchical, there is no sovereign other than God, and he invites all into common parliament with him, that is, to common prayer. In the church, the inner flaw of all this world's polities, our inevitable lust to dominate, is broken, because the One from whom we would here seek to wrest freedom cannot be dominated. In the church, all the baptized are invited to the table, where the host so gives himself to them that they have nothing more to wrest from him or from one another.

Does this mean that those not yet in the church are therefore not free? There is indeed a sense in which Christian theology must say they are not. Paul's encomia of freedom do not invoke a general character of the human race or of civil polities, but a reality experienced in the church; and that this world is in bondage is the unanimous opinion of Scripture.

27. Acts 2.

Yet longing for God is, after all, the very being of creatures, so that if we say that the world's freedom is mere inchoate longing for the God who is freedom, we attribute to at least some of the world's communities a predicate not to be despised. The freedom of this world's "free societies" and free persons is indeed inwardly self-destructive, but it is nonetheless real as what it is, and is to be treasured in all its fragility. The momentary spark of mutual liberation in a jury-room or political assembly — or at a dinner party or in a good argument — is a great blessing of the Creator. What we do not need and cannot have and should not want, is "the" free will — unless by that we simply mean God.

Thinking Reality

| | |

I

This chapter, like one other to follow, finds its continuing interlocutor in a piece of popular culture rather than in a certified thinker. I will, to be sure, call also on an erring philosopher and the theologian who corrected him.

The film *A Beautiful Mind* tells — beautifully — the somewhat fictionalized story of Princeton mathematician John Nash. After a brilliant beginning as a mathematician and a dismal beginning as an adult human being, he seems to achieve a sort of flourishing, as he is appointed to a prestigious post at M.I.T. and marries a beautiful and generally remarkable woman. Then he is disabled by schizophrenia, which is discovered simultaneously by moviegoers and the real (!) persons in the story to have been long at work. Conventional treatment with shock and continuing medication returns him to outpatient life, but also undoes his ability to do mathematics or make love to his wife. So he stops taking his medication, and his delusional friends and persecutors return.

Nash's triumph in the film is the ability which he then achieves to live with his delusions *as* delusions, and just so to reinhabit the real world: to speak memorably when accepting the Nobel Prize for his early work, to return to Princeton and there continue more modestly as a mathematician and — what he had never before been willing to take seriously — a teacher, and to live with his family. He is still "crazy," but knows it, and tells people to watch out for his craziness — approached by a representative of the Nobel Committee, he asks a by-standing student if she sees him too. But just so he has again a grip on reality, or at least a better grip than many supposedly more sane persons.

I have just referred to the "real" world. That is, of course, the problem for a fully delusional schizophrenic like Nash — and in one way or another for all of us. And it is an anthropological problem: the difficulty is with Nash, not with the things he sees and hears or thinks he does.[1] The question posed for this chapter is not whether there is anything that is real, or directly about what that might be like, but is about our grip on whatever *is* real[2] — though we will have to make one detour into the first question. Nash's problem was how to tell the difference between the ontic[3] status of, e.g., Russian agents pursuing him around Cambridge and that of his doctor, whom he first takes to be one of them; and when he comes to know the Russians are not real, his problem is how to know he really knows this. It is a problem that notoriously undoes both schizophrenics and philosophers.

"Reality" is perhaps a slightly different sort of notion than others taken up in this book, but is certainly an essential and problematic anthropological notion. "Get real," we may say, exhorting someone to conform his or her behavior or opinions to reality, and thereby asserting that the one addressed has lost his or her grip on things, that we are in a better situation in this respect, and that we are somehow able to *know* our situation is better. Merely listing these assertions is enough to make us worry about them.

1. If someone wishes to object that epistemology and metaphysics are not that easily separated, this is of course true. The distinction will, however, suffice for present purposes.

2. Perhaps the chapter should have been about "sanity," but after weighing the possibility I concluded that this was too broad a notion for the matter I wished to consider.

3. Not ontological or metaphysical.

As with the other essential anthropological notions discussed in this book, "real" is a term we are able to use after a fashion. We live as though criteria of reality were at hand, and for the most part do quite well at it. When Nash starts barring doors and windows against encircling Russian agents, we have the label "paranoia" ready to hand, sympathize with the "sick" man, and — having ourselves been deceived for much of the film — decide the Russians are not real.[4] If I see a stone, kick it, and feel nothing, I conclude the stone was an optical mistake. We can usually tell a schizophrenic when we talk to one. And we can do many more such things.

But then there are those moments when *criteria* are demanded, and are sometimes not found. Perhaps I do feel the conventionally appropriate sensation in my toe and yet for some reason still wonder whether this is not a tactile mistake to go with the optical one. It has been brilliantly argued that schizophrenia and the arts of modernity share a common structure, of "exigent introspection."[5] Yet the immediate experience of modernist art is its penetration into some "deeper" objective reality. What then of schizophrenia; is it too a vision of reality others do not see? A madman, it has been quipped, is not someone who is illogical, but someone who is *only* logical, and that seems right. But what then is the missing additional factor?

We for the most part handle the word "real" easily enough and for the most part rely on what we take to deserve the label, but — and here of course we come again to the theme of this book — we seem unable to think it. That is, in this case, we seem not to know what we are doing when we grant or refuse the compliment "real,"[6] or what a mistake would consist of, or how we would know a mistake had been made or how we would correct it.

4. Setting up this question is, by the way, brilliantly accomplished by the movie's writers, director, and actors.

5. Louis A. Sass, *Madness and Modernism: Insanity in the Light of Modern Art, Literature and Thought* (New York: Basic Books, 1992).

6. This is perhaps the place to note that this problem is to be distinguished from the circumstance that nearly all criteria are fuzzy, a circumstance marvelously unveiled as no problem by Wittgenstein.

The turning point of Nash's story has two determinants. One is the sheer power of a "beautiful" mind, to deal with unexpungeable delusion *as* delusion. Nash has the advantage over some schizophrenics, that his delusions are individualized and stable. One is the roommate and continuing best friend whose buoyant sociality supported socially crippled young Nash through graduate school, and who is later accompanied by a little-girl ward whose affection for Nash humanizes him when he most needs it. The other is the government spymaster who involves Nash in wildly satisfying work, in defense of the country against Russians plotting to plant a bomb in its heartland. A major step on Nash's way to reality is taken when he is appealed to by the little girl, stoops to caress her — now first perceived by moviegoers as a caressing of empty space — and tells her he can't play with her anymore. None of these *personae* go away, they just cease to determine his other behavior and beliefs: the spymaster still appears and exhorts Nash to renewed code-breaking efforts lest the bomb be set, but now is not obeyed; and the friend and ward come to say they miss him, but are regretfully turned away.

But intellectual strength alone does not do it. The turning point within the turning point is the moment when Nash's wife, Alicia, takes his hand and puts it to her face, and her hand to his, and says, "*This* is real." In his Nobel Prize address, Nash speaks of his lifelong quest for the reasons of things, for the mathematically formulable underlying dynamic of economic and analogous behavior, for a metaphysics to discipline his madness, for the reasons madness itself provided. He then directly addresses Alicia: "You are my reasons."[7]

Is love then the criterion of reality? If I love, am I in position to discern reality from illusion? Psychically or metaphysically? In the last chapter of this book, we will see that love is itself problematic. Can it bear the weight?

7. At which point the movie audience audibly weeps; the movie is among other things an old-fashioned tear-jerker.

II

Let us shift gears for the moment. Notoriously, much modern reflection on the methods and results of the sciences has concluded that the world as it presents itself to us is not the "real" world, but is merely the real world's effect on our particular cognitive equipment. The archetypical position of this type is that of John Locke. What "really" is out there, said Locke, are "substances" defined by those quantities that can appear in Newton's equations, by "the primary qualities." The shaped colors, scents, sounds, and touches that we actually apprehend are not in external reality; they are "secondary qualities," effects in us *caused* by those substances in their interactions. Knowing the world, in this scheme, is the functioning of an apparatus in us, which deals with stimuli from an intrinsically alien externality.

Of the eighteenth-century inheritors of Locke, it was two theologians, Bishop Berkeley and Jonathan Edwards, who saw most clearly that this part of his system would not do in its original version. I will follow Edwards, since I know him better.

Edwards was a great student and indeed fan of Locke. But he realized that Locke's distinction and ordering of "primary" and "secondary" qualities resulted not from Newtonian principle but, quite the contrary, from clinging to the inherited notion of "substances" within the inappropriate context of empirical science. If we wished to be drastically empirical, and still to regard some sorts of sense-data[8] as more intimate to reality than others, it would not be mass and geometry that we would take to define reality, but colors, sounds, etc. But in fact, the possibility of making this observation should lead us to abandon Locke's distinction altogether. And with it we should abandon the notion that the "ideas" in us are *caused* by things outside us that are not ideas; or alternatively, that ideas, however caused, are *in* us and *not outside* us, as if they were in a sort of smaller container within a larger one.[9]

8. Not, of course, Edwards's word.

9. Against some discussions of Edwards, it should be noted that such positions do not make him an "idealist." Idealism in any useful sense of the word was only possible after Kant. And Edwards thought of himself as a radical empiricist.

Edwards saw that it is precisely the notion that reality causes our perceptions of it which posits a gap between reality and cognition, and compels us to otiose attempts to bridge the gap. I am said to receive what is out there by and into something in here, but how do I receive the reception itself, so as to know that it succeeds? If, on the other hand, we see that the very distinction between ideas in us and substances out there is a fiction, the problem disappears.

If Edwards's argument, or perhaps one of its more recent analogues, is right, it has a double effect. One is that the notion of material reality as composed of material "substances," active chunks of stuff, is undone, yielding an ontology more amenable to the picture drawn by contemporary physics — and indeed also by Newtonian physics, if only more thinkers of the time had noticed. What is there, according to present report from the theorists, is vectored occurrences of various sorts, within an architecture specifiable only by mathematics that cannot be represented; this is a reality very unlike any antique picture of "material substances."

The other, closely related and more important to our present concern, is that the distinction between "in" us and "outside of" us disappears; our percepts are "in" neither supposed container, they just are. We see, hear, touch, and taste what we see, hear, touch, and taste, and that is all there is to be said about the matter; our percepts are not caused by something we do not see, taste, touch, or hear. As Edwards insists, it is far from his intention to abolish the notions of material reality and of the laws that govern its behavior, only to demythologize them. Material things are not causes of our experience, i.e., little gods; they are exactly and only what we perceive, whether with or without devices[10] to strengthen our perceptions.

It will be seen that what Edwards has done is radicalize Locke in a direction that has sometimes led to modernity's less profound sorts of idealism. What preserves Edwards from this fate? It is that Edwards knows about God. *God* is the cause of our "ideas"; that they are

10. As a science buff, Edwards of course knew about the scientific apparatus of his time, which was quite sufficient to pose any metaphysically important questions.

posited by his creative thinking and not by ours constitutes the otherness of what we perceive and know. God's knowing and willing constitute the "substance" of things out there, if, as Edwards says, "we must needs" find some use for this word. Thus we are no more the instigators of our experience of the world then are those mythic material substances; we no more need be idealists than we need be materialists. God is Creator and we are creatures.

So what is there finally?[11] There is a universal society of minds, God and creatures, with their various cognitions. Our percepts and the objects of the names or descriptions we find we need to use, insofar as these are *of* reality distinguishable from the mere minds themselves, constitute the intersubjectivity of the society of minds, by virtue of which they are separate minds yet in communion. And this state of affairs obtains because minds and what they perceive and know are all willed posits in the mind of the head of this society, in the mind of God.

Edwards would thus be that currently much dreaded sort of heretic, a "panentheist,"[12] except for having abolished the "in/out" distinction altogether, and replacing it with a biblical way of conceiving our otherness from God. God wills to know a world, and this world rather than some other; thus the world is willed reality and God is reality that does not need to be willed.

Finally, it may be noted that this analysis of modernity's typical error about the implications of science, and the previous narrative of John Nash's madness, are not so unrelated as may at first appear. For it seems that schizophrenia is a specifically modern ailment; despite meticulous record-keeping by premodern observers, its symptoms are not described before the modern period.[13] That is, they are not described before the time when we began thinking of something-we-know-not-what as what is "really" "out" there, and of ourselves as "subjects" to be known by — ever more stringent — introspection.

11. Here of course begins the detour early announced.

12. One for whom all things other than God are "in" God in such fashion that the distinction between God and other reality threatens to become uncontrollable.

13. To this, see Sass, ad loc.

III

But why does God will that something other than himself be real? Edwards's answer, and that of the general Christian tradition, is that it is because God loves — and from this point on, I will no longer be reporting Edwards in particular. God does not need anything other than himself to have an object of love, since he is triune; but if in fact he wills other things to love, that settles the matter. Notoriously, there is no demanding further reasons of love. Why Israel instead of Egypt? Why this lover instead of some other? Why you and me as the elect instead of unbelieving Jones over there? Why a world instead of no world? Why does a child love shrimp but not scallops?

What is real is real because Love loves it. The proposition, to be sure, poses an awful question about those things that are manifestly both real and evil, but that is not the concern here — for which the author is grateful. Other questions must, however, be posed. If the world is truly other than us because God antecedently perceives it, how is it other for God? Who rescues him from being what he rescues us from being, a solipsist, a dreamer of reality rather than someone with a grip on it?

If God's love were appropriately evoked by the mere theistic proposition, "God loves," then the position so far sketched would indeed make the world God's dream merely. But the theistic proposition is not in fact adequate, for the real God is Father, Son, and Spirit; his love is first and foundationally the love *between* the Father and the Son, enabled by and indeed constituted in the self-giving of the Spirit to both. Thus God's love is intersubjective without needing to be the love of what is other than God, and indeed is consequent to its own intersubjectivity: the Father is the Father, who begets the Son and breathes the Spirit, ontologically prior to there being simply God,[14] of whom we may theistically say that "he loves us" — or knows us or whatever else God does. Further, it is an ancient and ecumenical

14. This is the great and in its own context true and indispensable contention of much modern Orthodox theology.

maxim of Christian theology: what God is and what God does or has are distinguishable only notionally. The God who loves us *is* love. And so the Godhead that is love is itself *founded* in intersubjectivity, for there is no Godhead antecedent to the Father's begetting the Son and breathing the Spirit.

Nor is God's knowing appropriately evoked by the theistic proposition, "God knows." There is an alternative proper name for the second identity of God; we may equally affirm: the real God is Father, *Word,* and Spirit. And God's knowing is first and foundationally the Father's hearing the Word that he himself speaks, enabled by and indeed constituted in the Freedom — here another alternative name — which the Spirit gives the Father and the Son. And again, by the maxim just invoked God *is* knowing, or as we are more likely to say, truth. Thus Godhead as truth is founded in intersubjectivity, precisely as he is as love.

In God, therefore, that reality is known and reality is loved are aspects of the one fact of the triune intersubjectivity. God cannot know something without loving it, or love something without knowing it. Moreover, what God knows or loves other than God is created by the knowing or loving. Therefore, with respect to God's love and knowledge of creatures, the point just made is not the trivial point that something absolutely unknown could hardly be loved, nor something absolutely unregarded attract cognition. The situation is more drastic: that God knows a creature is to love it; and that he loves a creature is to know it.

We, to be sure, are not God and do not create what we know and love by our knowing or loving it. Thus we do seem to some extent able to be indifferent to something we know, and to be ignorant of something we love. But this "ability" is a character of fallen humanity, and it is our attempt to act on it that posits the gulf between our knowing and what we know, which modernity has otiosely labored to bridge, and on the brink of which special sufferers like Nash in fact teeter.

There is, as we learned from Edwards, no "substance" to creatures but God's grasp of them, whether we think of that grasp as his loving or his knowing. If creatures existed in any way independently of God's grip on them, they could perhaps be grasped otherwise than as God does it. But as it is, if others than God are to know or love creatures, those others must act in some analogy to the way in which God does this. Thus any attempt to know a creature disinterestedly can at best be only a temporary tactic, such as that for the moment adopted by the sciences, and at worst and more likely a sinful objectification. And any attempt to love a creature ignorantly can at best be only amusing play, and at worst and more likely sinful egotism.

That any reliable grasp of what is must be somehow loving, is the deep reason why the things we know as other than ourselves are truly other. It is the deep reason why our percepts and the objects of our concepts are not merely *located* in us, and why those that are in fact so located are delusions, why too exigent *intro*spection[15] can open to an even schizophrenic loss of grip. For, if we may for the moment speak as if there could be love that was not knowing or knowing that was not love, even such love, unlike such knowing, could not be its own sole object. A relation to myself can meaningfully be called love only if I indeed love my neighbor as myself. For though it is sometimes supposed that Scripture's famous mandate makes self-love a standard which our love for the other is to emulate, the relation in Scripture works the other way; Scripture contains no mention of self-love except as a foil for love of the other. The object of love is always other than the love.[16]

It will perhaps not quite do to say that if we "only love" we will merely thereby get real. But because God is the God he is and is as this God the Creator of all things, if we do not love we indeed can have no firm grip on anything.

15. The phrase is intended to capture the paradigmatic and doomed venture of William James, in his great and itself delusional *Principles of Psychology.*

16. The deep problematics of this statement will be partially explored in the last chapter.

IV

The argument just concluded is still too abstract. Alicia did not simply affirm her love for John, she touched him and made him touch her. Love that is not somehow bodily is a mere figment, for we must have the intersubjective material world to be both other than one another and able to come together with one another. Nor does the mere fact of an environing material world enable love; I must myself be a body and you likewise, if we are to love.

Alicia touched and said, "This is real." Her statement should remind believers of other gestures and words: "This is my body"; "This is my blood." It should make us think of "real presence."

There is no love without embodiment; Nash would — in the conception of the film — not have recovered if Alicia had not at just that moment *touched* him and helped him touch her. If the screenwriters had been less sophisticated, they would surely have had Alicia say, as they touched, "I am there for you." And indeed the annoying cliché captures the point we need here: the body is the person's *availability* to others and to him or herself.[17] Were I disembodied, you could not find me, to love me or indeed to hate me. Touching John and helping him touch her, Alicia gives herself to be present for him, to be the object of his love.

Neither can God love without embodiment, without mutual availability. We must of course immediately note that this is not because we can reason from our necessities to his; indeed the argument, as we will see in a moment, goes the other way around. If there is to be love between the Father and the Son, the Son must be somehow available to the Father, must be, that is, somehow embodied for him. In the history that God in fact creates, the Son is available to the Father as the embodied human, Jesus. But also if there were a different creation, or none at all, the Son would somehow be available to the Father — though about that "somehow" we may not further speculate.

17. I may refer again to my *Systematic Theology* (New York: Oxford University Press, 1997-99), vol. 1, pp. 204-6.

We have already argued: our grip on reality must conform, in our fashion, to God's, if it is not forever to be problematic. In the present context that means: our grip on reality will only be secured if God gives the Son, as whom his knowledge and love are embodied for himself, to be embodied also for us. Our grip on reality is and can only be participation in God's grip on his creation. When it comes down to it, we would float free from reality, were not the Son there for us to touch, did he not direct us to a body and say, "This is *my* body."

Finally therefore, the act by which we grasp reality is that by which we obey the institution of the Eucharist. We are to give thanks to God for all his blessings, specifically including the sacrifice of the Son, and we are to commune with God and our fellows in that thanksgiving by seizing upon the embodiment of that Son, by taking and eating and drinking his real availability. And our various other perceivings and conceivings in the plural, by which we hope to grasp reality, succeed to the precise extent to which they occur in some analogy to our actions in the Eucharist.

We of course make many difficulties for ourselves about the Real Presence. We do this because we suppose there is some other criterion of reality, by which the reality of the Son's presence is to be measured. There is none; rather, our grasp of the Son's real body and blood is the criterion of all our other attempts to grasp something real.

It remains only to specify the analogy between our cognitive success in Eucharist and our cognitive attempts elsewhere — at this point necessarily rather too homiletically. We grasp reality when our labors to do so are an act of obedience to some invitation of God, analogous to the invitation "Do this. . . ." In our fallen state, this criterion is more easily instanced negatively: since God does not invite us to kill, experimentation on human embryos is not just morally wicked, it must infallibly lead to cognitive disaster. We grasp reality when we receive it as God's gift for our good. Melanchthon's maxim, "To know God is to know his benefits," has been much misused, but if we take it as intended, it applies not only to God but to his creatures. We truly grasp any creature when we grasp what good God makes it for — which, for currently unavoidable instance, accounts for the rancorous sterility into which biology has devolved, in its refusal to take account of purpose. We grasp reality when we are touched lovingly by it.[18]

18. That these claims are much in the style of Charles Peirce's "pragmatism" has been made clear to me by the writings and conversation of Peter Ochs.

Thinking Wickedness

| | |

I

This chapter is begun on the Monday following the terrorist destruction of part of New York City, the merciless random killing of thousands who worked or lived there, and the breaking of endlessly intricate webs of love, as of virtue, talent, and achievement. In the days after the event we experienced a public use of language not heard in polite circles for some years: the terrorists are "evil" or "wicked" or just plain "bad." At least for the moment, we seem willing indeed to "impose our values" on some who do not share them, even to punish them for acting on other values, and to entertain other ways of treating bad behavior than by therapy — one reads no proposals of "help" to conspirators who may be captured.[1] We have not reached the point where we speak publicly of "sin," and in discourse outside the church that may be just as well; in the following we will use this word also. To be sure, on some university campuses and in other remaining Leninist enclaves people do discuss even this outrage within a schema of moral equivalence between Western misdeeds and third-world response; we will come back to that. And of course one can make no predictions about what the language of public discourse will be by the time these lines are read.

1. Though one must suppose that in some quarters they are being made.

The reason for the at least momentary public reversion to the vocabulary of evil is plain: it is the only language with resources adequate to characterize such an act or those who did it. Nor will any consideration of mitigating circumstances suffice to eliminate need for this language. America's eyes certainly harbor beams we should remove before we look too minutely for motes elsewhere, and the Islamic world for whom the terrorists claim to act harbors appalling injustice, some of which may be partly our fault; but these things neither justify nor explain the deed. The killers and their handlers, financiers, and protectors have done a wicked thing, and at least for the moment we recognize this judgment as dispositive.

Now these malefactors were and are not animals or angels, but people, from which circumstance we should learn that people do not always merely make mistakes or suffer from one or another trauma, but sometimes just do bad things. Moreover, once the language is employed, it is hard not to think that at least some of the wicked things people do are such that the adjective properly transfers from the deed to the person. Finally, if people are sometimes wicked, the possibility of wickedness must be a human dispositional property, so that the concept is at least insofar a concept of general application. "Wickedness" thus appears as an anthropological predicate, and one we are, as of this writing, sometimes driven actually to use.[2]

But there is a problem: What *sort* of anthropological predicate is wickedness? The Western church and Western society have long been theoretically and practically troubled by a felt dilemma in our use of the notion. Stating the dilemma in the Aristotelian language of the theological controversy I am about to adduce: Does "wickedness" point to the human "substance" or to an "accident" thereof? As we will see, it seems to fit neither rubric, and that will display our problem for this chapter.

I am not sure whether or not the problem obtains for all who speak or can speak of wickedness. But it certainly obtains for Chris-

2. When liberation from late-modern ideology allows us momentarily to gather our wits about us.

tian discourse, and for the culture once shaped by it. And it has important public moral involvements.

Since the particular difficulties with thinking wickedness I am about to describe occur especially within Christian discourse and its secularizations, they are insofar analogous to our problem with "freedom." And as in that case, there is an assortment of possible historical exemplifications. Within the scope of my historical information, an especially straightforward display of the puzzle is provided by Lutheran theology in the period immediately following the Reformation.[3] The Lutheran theologians asked: When we say that "after the fall" humans are sinful just as the persons they are, never mind what deeds they commit,[4] are we talking about something that belongs to our nature or substance, that is, to what we must be to be ourselves, or about an accident, that is, a characteristic with or without which we could remain identical with ourselves? About something we necessarily are or about something we unnecessarily — even if invariably — are?

The distinction is a commonsensical one, as most Aristotelian distinctions are: were I at this moment of writing to cease to be mammalian, the writing of this essay would cease because *I* would have ceased; were my hair instantly to turn white, I could carry on writing as the same one I was before. Thus some predicates of any real thing can be seen as belonging to its "substance," in the sense that without them the thing would not be at all, while others, "accidents," can come and go less portentously.

Moreover, the Aristotelian sorting of categories makes the disjunction exclusive; anything real is either substance or accident. Entities thought to have their own self-contained integrity, like "the

3. To the controversy and the following generally, including the citations from Luther and others, see the long discussion and adjudication in the latest (1577) of the Lutheran Confessions, the *Formula of Concord,* Solid Declaration, I.

4. Their language for this was, of course, "original sin." The usual problems with this concept need not bother us here. Original sin is wickedness that somehow pertains not only to a person's acts but to the person him or herself, and does so without regard to particular derelictions; so much is plainly a phenomenon observed by faith, and further aspects of the doctrine need not concern us here.

house on the corner" or "John Smith," or to be inalienable components of such an entity, fall under the rubric of substance. An accident[5] — like "the white color of that house" or "John Smith's courage" — so inheres in some substance that it might be alienated from the substance without destruction thereof, whereas the accident itself would not occur at all without this inherence.

The Lutheran argument broke out around the teachings of Michael Illyricus Flacius, the most unrelenting of those for whom the very words of Luther's theology were indispensable.[6] Luther had thrown some very heavy rhetoric at late medieval scholasticism's indeed rather feeble characterizations of original sin, using among other resources the language of nature and substance: fallen humanity is "by nature sinful and unclean"; original sin is "nature-sin";[7] our nature is "corrupted in all its capacities and propensities." Indeed, Luther could say to the fallen human, "Your birth, your nature and your whole substance is sin. . . ." To be sure, he followed that with "that is, is sinful . . . ," but the second-thought shift from noun to adjective hardly much mitigates so very forcefully stated a proposition.

Whatever Luther's own intent, Flacius drew from Luther a deliberately provocative doctrine: that with fallen humans ". . . original sin is their substance, because the rational soul, and especially those of its powers that are both most noble and most integral to [the soul's] substance . . . , which once were so wonderfully shaped and directed[8] that they were a true image of God . . . , are now by Satan's trick so inverted that they are actually an . . . image of Satan."[9] This was too much for most of his fellow Lutherans, who said it contradicted both the doctrine of creation and the promises of redemption. If wickedness is the fallen human's substance, then it cannot be rooted out without rooting out the person, that is, without undoing God's cre-

5. Which here does not mean "accidental."

6. And the pioneer of modern church history and the soul of Protestant resistance during the opening religious wars when all seemed lost.

7. *Natursünde.*

8. *"formatae"*

9. Flacius, *Clavis scripturae sacrae,* II:482.

ation and the object of the promises. If wickedness pertains substantially to the human person, then the Incarnation is impossible: the infinitely good Son could not assume human nature without just thereby abolishing it.[10]

So what were they to say instead? So long as it is agreed that anything real is either substance or accident,[11] if original sin is real and is not substance, it has to be accident. And that is the doctrine on which majority Lutheranism settled: "If one inquires whether original sin is substance . . . or accident, it is without qualification . . . to be taught . . . that sin is not substance but accident."[12]

The difficulty is, that accidents can come and go without ontologically deep disruption, which does not seem to be the case with original sin as Christian theology and piety otherwise treat it. John Smith's courage may one day fail him, however strong our reasons to rely on it, and its restoration may be hard or easy; moreover, both loss and restoration will usually be partial. Is it the same with his "original" wickedness? If sin is indeed "without qualification" an accident, one would think that moral exhortation or severe penitential disciplines — or now therapy or meditation or whatever — should suffice at least to control it; and then it becomes hard to see why the fallenness of humanity should require so drastic a step as the Incarnation and death of God the Son.

The theologians who opposed Flacius plainly worried — at least subliminally — that such conclusions could be drawn from their teaching, and sought to prevent this with — after all — a flood of qualifications. Original sin may be an accident, but it is such a remarkable, "cancerous," accident that it perverts the "whole nature, person and essence of man . . . at its ground."[13] The intent of Luther's extreme language had been, they said, to make clear "what a truly horrid sort of quality or 'accident' [sin] is, by which human nature is not only polluted but is so deeply perverted that nothing pure

10. A position, by the way, not unknown in Christian history.

11. And all parties emphatically did agree to that.

12. *Formula of Concord,* 7, 57.

13. *Formula of Concord,* 7, 53.

or unspoiled remains in it. . . ."[14] The renewed trouble is: if such language as the "whole [human] essence . . . at its ground" or "nothing . . . remains," is taken seriously, the difference between the orthodox position and that of Flacius becomes merely a linguistic stipulation.[15] So the orthodox Lutheran solution only displays the difficulty more clearly: if personal wickedness is substance, it is ineradicable; if it is accident, it should be more easily eradicated than Christian teaching allows to be the case.

And a further problem has doubtless been glimpsed along the way. For our instance of the dilemma about wickedness, we have taken the Lutheran dispute about "original sin." But original sin is a corruption to which all are supposed to be subject and not just specifically wicked persons, whereas we started out with the differentiating wickedness of the recent terrorists. Have we not slipped away from our matter? If ". . . is wicked" means the same when said of the terrorists as it does when said of rescuers among the slain, there is little point in saying it about the terrorists.

There is a connection: if "original" wickedness were truly "without qualification" an "accident," this second problem could be easily solved: most people could be thought to shed personal wickedness when properly situated or resolved, and the rest would be the truly wicked ones. But as it is, we have to ask: What is the difference between the wickedness of true miscreants and the "original" wickedness of ordinary middling-virtuous folk? Why are we not all on the most-wanted list?

II

The puzzles just formulated demand solution, for the thinking they impede is greatly needed. It makes a difference in the life of the church and the world whether we think of wickedness as a substance

14. *Formula of Concord,* 7, 62.

15. The orthodox Lutherans were not Flacians in the same way Augustine notoriously was not a modalist: because they said they were not.

or as an accident — or perhaps as something else. And it makes a difference whether we are or are not able plausibly and clearly to distinguish between original wickedness and the wickedness of those society must turn from their ways, by force if necessary.

Interpretation of human wrongness as an accident — of course not now often with that language — determines the daily life of the late-modern West, penetrating and indeed radiating from the churches also. It is not only certain office-holders who can be described as "Teflon-coated," in that their malefactions stick only loosely to their persons; we are all more or less impaired in this way. The "therapeutic" society could not obtain were we to regard our unsatisfactory behavior as coming from our "real" selves: with certain sinister exceptions, people do not go to a healer to be cured of themselves, only of something accidental to their selves.

The erstwhile churches that now take it as their mission to administer as much or little religion as drop-ins can tolerate without inconvenience, could not be content with this role if they thought there was anything seriously wrong with all those people. In the more "mainline churches" also, and in "progressive" Catholicism, one lately has heard remarkably little of redemption by Christ or of the eschatologically transformed existence he gains for us, and surely the reason is that people and clergy have been aware of no problem it would take Christ to deal with. "Peace and justice issues" are surely vital in themselves, but they are poor substitutes for death and Resurrection, unless there is no other death than organic termination and so no need for resurrection.

So far this modernity seems quite cheery. Yet there is a dark side to it and to its churchly source and victim. The Flacian alternative is simultaneously enacted: even as we disavow our transgressions, we are not sure there is anything to us but evil. When a late-forties group of college sophomores who had read Schopenhauer went about chanting, to a sort of plain-tone, "All is evil, nothing is worth striving for," we meant to be outrageous; but that was then, now there are entire territories and social classes where there would be nothing remarkable about the sentiment.

Actual nihilism is surely impossible for God's human creatures, but it must indeed be possible for us to live by nihilism's anticipated or even invoked advent, since many do just that; life in the foreshadow of nihilism is perhaps the best description of late-modernism or postmodernism. And there *are* now those who go to physicians to be cured of themselves; there are even wicked persons who bring others for the purpose.

In the church, modernity's dark side appears as "antinomianism" — historians' label for a heresy that emerged within the same early Lutheranism as Flacius. If personal wickedness is ineradicable, why rail against it? Why "preach the law"?, as one put it then. Fallen humanity will do what it does, and we must simply turn its "salvation" over to God — the scare-quotes are there because, of course, under these suppositions we cannot know what damnation or then salvation would be. I do not necessarily delight in your "lifestyle," but since it is yours, love requires that I leave you to it. I do not necessarily delight in my own lifestyle either, but that's the way I was made and I need to love myself too — and we will be saved by grace in any case. So runs the theology of much of the late-modern church. Despite its appearance it is a dark theology indeed.

And what of the distinction between all of us being wicked and some of us being wicked? It will not do to think it quantitatively; terrorists, for current instance, are not merely somewhat worse than the rest of us. Doubtless it is universal "original sin" that constitutes the possibility of what evil persons do, and we will not understand them until we have been frightened by our own potentialities;[16] yet the move from possibility to actuality cannot in this context be conceived as development or emergence.

Here too the position taken has serious public consequences. The day after the attack on New York, a child of privilege at an Ivy League university, emulating some of her professors more baldly than they may have wished, said to an acquaintance, "We kill Iraqis all the time.

16. G. K. Chesterton's detective priest, Father Brown, is the great authority at this point.

Why shouldn't Muslims kill some of us sometimes?" United States forces indeed sometimes kill Iraqis.[17] Without original wickedness, including ours, this would not happen. Perhaps even in this fallen world it would not happen were we wiser. But none of these considerations establish the moral equivalence supposed by the student, *unless* we cannot tell the difference between the corruption of us all, with its lamentable consequences, and the ability to commit random mass murder for the sheer sake of civilizational revenge. In fact, large tracts of Western elite culture *can* no longer tell the difference.

It is dogma in much of academia, following those particular postmodernists whom in this and the next chapter I will refer to as Nietzsche's French epigones, that all human intercourse is violence.[18] According to Nietzsche, whenever we confront one another, each of us incorporates — under various levels of concealment — the "will to power," which thus figures in this thinking as the human substance very much in Flacius' sense. The difference is that Flacius deplores this supposed deep truth about us, and Nietzsche "celebrates" it. Nietzsche's French epigones claim to reject all "metanarratives," but in fact do posit a metaphysical absolute: violence is the one inescapable fact, the infinite to which all good-faith tracings of finite beings' intercourse must lead.

But if all human intercourse is violence in a metaphysical sense, and so in the same sense with all, then giving[19] food to feed the Afghani people — as the United States has been doing for decades — is "really" imperialist violence if only someone declares it to be. Then accepting this food and preparing the destruction of the givers are again equal acts of violence, and both no otherwise violent than the giving. Then the death and destruction in the south of Manhattan cannot finally be judged in moral terms at all, no moral distinctions

17. And who knows what will have happened by the time this is read!

18. Friedrich Nietzsche is indeed the great fountain of this particular sort of what he himself called "nihilism." For the postmodern version, see, e.g., Jacques Derrida, *Writing and Difference* (Chicago: University of Chicago, 1978).

19. Picking a gift for the instance at this point is appropriate; the impossibility of actually giving anything is a great theme of such ideology.

being available, but only perhaps in aesthetic ones, as did the German anti-composer who said it was "a work of art." Then the insufferable sophomore earlier quoted is a person of fine sensibility.

III

If we assume Flacius is using the terms of traditional metaphysics in the traditional ways, his propositions about sin are patently absurd, at least as items of Christian theology. Therefore, since Flacius was a person of high intelligence and an intransigent Christian, we should probably not read his propositions that way: almost certainly a project of revisionary metaphysics was preparing itself under his provocations. To be sure, his opponents did not notice this, and perhaps neither did he.

It is not an exercise for this volume, to reconstruct Flacius' latent new metaphysics, but we may take his cue. With persons, the traditional metaphysical notion of substance has functioned to specify personal continuity across time: when my hair turns color I remain myself; if I become an insect I will no longer be myself; if I lose my mind, people may wonder how to speak of the matter — is Jenson, after all, "himself"? We must note that this thinking conceives self-identity as constituted in a kind of self-enclosure, a bounded and indeed barricaded keep of certain possessed identifications; a thing's self-identity is what it is "in" itself as opposed to what about it is in response to what is not in itself. The most likely explanation of Flacius' initially absurd assertions is that Flacius had a notion of personal continuity that located it otherwise than within such an impermeably bounded self. Be that as it may, it may be apparent to hindsight that the difficulties we have been tracing are due to traditional metaphysics' construal of self-identity as self-enclosure and self-possession.

If faith's grasp of reality is right, and despite theologians' frequent failure to note it, nothing within a creature can constitute its self-continuity through time; Ibsen's Button-maker will find no core to any created onion. Creatures are at every step contingent on

God, that is, on another than themselves[20] — it is contingencies all the way down.

We should appropriate the fundamental insight of Thomas Aquinas: with creatures — as not with God — *what* I am and *that* I am are two distinct facts; we could know everything *about* a supposed creature that omniscience itself could know, and still not know whether that creature in fact exists.[21] If we take time into Aquinas's proposition,[22] we will say: we could know everything about what a creature has been up until now, including that it has existed up until now, and still have merely therein no guarantee that anything now exists in continuity with that former identity. Also my self-continuity across time is wholly contingent on something I am not.[23]

Nor, if this is right, can there be any impermeable boundary between what I substantially am and what I accidentally am. The point about the traditional notion of accidents is that they are wholly subject to time, they are not in themselves perduring realities, whereas substances perdure for greater or lesser times in the power of their own constituting forms. But Christian faith sees each creature as such and in its identity with itself as wholly subject to time: nothing in me-myself-and-mine conduces to my perdurance; I have no intrinsic grip on myself. If we were to persist in the substance/accident schema, Christian theology would finally have to say that only God — and that in a peculiar triune way — is substance, and that human selves are simply accidental, not only in the sense that any one of them might not have been, but that when there contingently is a human self its accidentality is the very mode of its being.[24]

20. It can be said that God too is contingent, indeed absolute Contingency, but in the triune perichoresis it is himself to whom he is contingent.

21. *De esse et essentia,* v,44-48.

22. Which Thomas himself does not seem to have done. It is perhaps his only serious error, in general to have handled the eternity/time distinction uncritically.

23. Thus Jean-Paul Sartre, having eliminated God from the metaphysical scene, could write a sort of novel, *La Nausée,* on the supposition that its central character could at any moment be something other than himself.

24. Which is surely a good reason not to persist in the substance/accident schema.

Doubtless the substance/accident schema would not have endured so long were there *no* use for it. It is of course convenient sometimes to distinguish between what I must be to be myself and everything else I am. But not every commonsensical distinction can with truth be recruited as a metaphysical principle; and Christian insight should prevent us from so recruiting this one.

IV

We have come in this chapter to the place at which each chapter has arrived: we must refer outside ourselves in order successfully to think those notions by which we think ourselves. More particularly to this chapter, we must learn to think our selves as dependent precisely on our permeability to others than ourselves. Yet more particularly to this chapter, we must learn to understand our personal wickedness as a — perverse — phenomenon of that permeability; and we must learn to understand the wickedness of specific persons as a phenomenon at specific nodes of the web of mutual permeability.

As creatures, it is to the Creator we must refer to if we wish to understand our contingent self-identity and the contexts within which we are permeable. And that is, we again must refer to the triune God, and to the utter mutual contingency of Father, Son, and Spirit. As we have said before — no doubt to satiety — all there is to being the Father is being the Father of the Son, and all there is to being the Son is being the Son of this Father, and all there is to being the Spirit is being the Spirit of this Father for this Son; thus the triune God's personal being is constituted precisely in perfect contingency to — as one now says — the other. The wonder that God is, is the wonder that these contingencies are perfectly mutual, that Father, Son, and Spirit are but one God, so that with God contingency to the other is identical with *not* being an accident. God and only God can, if one likes to put it so, be substance precisely by virtue of infinite permeability.

We can rely further on earlier discussion. God creates by taking time within his eternal time for others than the three who are himself. That is, in the present context, to be a creature is to be located within and permeable to the triune communal environment. I am identical with myself across time, both now and in the Kingdom, not by virtue of what is within me but by virtue of what I am within, by virtue of specific location in the unbroken life of Father, Son, and Spirit. I am identical with myself across time precisely because I am no "substance" to defend itself against God's intent for me, because I am entirely permeable to his eternal community and just so reliably located at a place within it. I perdure because the perdurance of the divine life takes account of me: because the Father calls me into being by name and does not fall silent; because within the body of the Son I am communally located at such and such a crossing of mutual personal relations and not elsewhere and because the body of the Son has eternal life; and because the Spirit who is always Future inspires in me a unique complex of dynamisms, natural and charismatic.

Reference to the church, the body of Christ, signals that it is not only the triune community to which I am permeable. There could not have been just one creature, and therefore I belong also to created communities. I am myself by virtue of location in and openness to not only Father, Son, and Spirit, but within a family, a tribe, a nation, a community of work, perhaps indeed the church, and so on and on. *Mutatis mutandis,* what was said above about my determination within the triune life can be said about my determination within any of these. And in this plurality of communal contexts occurs, in brute contingency, my sinfulness.

No one can serve two masters; I will inevitably serve one and so hate other claimants. Original sin is hatred of God as the other side of loyalty to other masters; and that I indeed have other masters is sin's originality to my person. It is as we are in our persons permeable to our communal contexts, that hatred of God and by inevitable association of at least some of our fellows[25] is personal to us. There *should* of course be no conflict between loyalty within the triune community

25. Why do the wicked invariably hate the Jews? Because they are the people of God.

and loyalty within created communities; there should be no possibility of a creature being my master, since the overlapping communities by which we are ourselves, are either God himself or God's creatures. But conceivable or not the conflict has happened and does happen.

The oddity — within the terms of substance vs. accident — of "original" wickedness, that it both is and is not integral to my person, is thus clarified. Until "the nations walk by [the] light" of the Lamb, so that the triune community and all created community are indeed at one, I will have other possible masters than God, and in the contingency of the fall love some of them instead of God. This evil is indeed both certain and a feature of the permeability to others by which I am a person at all. Yet it is variable: today I may love Mammon, tomorrow ostentatious poverty, and death on the third. And when all communities are brought into the community of the Kingdom, I will be cured without being eradicated.

That some are wicked in a special sense is also accounted for. Continuing with the instance that instigated this chapter, a terrorist — contingently! — appears at a *particular* overlap of communities, at a particular node of mutual permeability. Each of us lives at and from a unique node in a cat's-cradle of mutualities. Moreover, each of us lives within communities some others do not inhabit at all; and with respect to the particular possible twistings of hatred for God and humanity that constitute wickedness, all communities are *not* alike. At every location in the web of communities, the crossings present the possibility of sin, but some of them open into nothingness. Still continuing with modern terrorism as our case, the perpetrators emerge within specific communities and not others, and at specific crossings of those communities with others.

The wickedness of the terrorist is his or her infliction of death as sheer revenge and provocation, like the robber who having been given the money and having an open retreat shoots the storekeeper for good measure. "Just"[26] war-making or police violence kills or dis-

26. We need not here argue whether there *is* such a thing as just war-making, or whether Christians can participate in it, to make the immediately relevant point.

ables those who must be removed to save the peace, and sometimes unavoidably the harmless around them; it does the first because it must be done and strives to reduce the second. In contrast, it is — again — the contingency, the sheer gratuity of the terrorist's harm-doing that makes it a wickedness. And this sort of gratuity appears when the hatred of God that constitutes original sin encounters at its node in the web of communities no face but itself.

In classical Augustinian doctrine, evil is pure absence, the darkness where the light of being runs out. The devil is the personal reality of evil: thus there is nothing to him but his deficiencies. The wicked person is the one whose encounter with nothingness in all connections of his or her permeability is such as to make emptiness his or her longed-for milieu, the devil his or her true master. Precisely at this point we must note the role of false religion: those who attacked New York did so, if their instructions were carried out, with prayer on their lips.

I have elsewhere laid it down, that sin must not be explained.[27] I hope I have not with these considerations violated that rule. Nor, I trust, have I here proposed a determinism; the issue of freedom and bondage remains exactly as analyzed in an earlier chapter. It remains that the terrorist — or the abortionist, or the sheerly heedless real estate magnate, or . . . — does the evil that he does because he chooses to do so.

27. *Systematic Theology,* vol. 2 (New York: Oxford University Press, 1999), pp. 113-14.

Thinking Love

| | |

I

You always hurt the one you love,
The one you shouldn't hurt at all.
You always take the sweetest rose,
And crush it till the petals fall.

Each chapter in this book has taken some philosopher or theologian, or several of them, as interlocutors. The author of the once popular song just cited does not perhaps qualify as a major thinker, and his verses will be duly supplemented by a passage from Hegel and by dispute with the group I call Nietzsche's French epigones.[1] But the verse very well displays the romanticism that has determined the West's interpretation of love through much of our history, and displays also the aporia of that interpretation, which are the matter of this chapter.

It seems indeed well established by experience: "You always hurt the one you love." And the hurt is always inherently fatal; rose petals

1. I have of course reference above all to Lyotard, Foucault, and Derrida. It may be a matter of justice to note that these persons usually make sense, as their American epigones-in-turn usually do not.

fall. But how and why is that? Vice versa, the knightly lover sung by the troubadours longed not for sexual congress with his lady — who was supposed to be above all that — but to be allowed to risk his life for her. How and why is that?

From both sides love and death are in our culture closely associated: the lover kills the beloved and the lover dies for the beloved. Centuries of Western romanticism are summed up in the title of one song of Richard Wagner: *Liebestod,* "Love-death." As of this writing, the movie *Moulin Rouge* has just provided an update of the ancient syndrome: at the finale, the poet and the courtesan find love that will be "without end" precisely in that she dies in his arms — if he could have simultaneously died in hers, that would have been better yet, but the script writers needed him to survive as the autobiographical narrator.

Much very recent culture, of course, eschews such romanticism; *Moulin Rouge* was a sensation just because it renewed it, and it could do this only by intruding multiple layers of pastiche and resultant irony. But in turning against romanticism — at least outwardly — the culture of suspicion ends with nothing at all to say about love, except as some postmodernist manifestations wholly *identify* it with death — a phenomenon to which I will return.

So what is this connection of love and death? To discover that, we must note love's dual nature: to love is to *give* and to *desire.*

To love is not to give something; it is to give myself. I may indeed give gifts in the plural to my beloved; but these, if indeed they are gifts of love, are mere tokens of the only thing I really have to give and the only thing the beloved can really receive, which is myself. If I forget a remembrance cherished between my beloved and me, it is not the absent roses that are mourned, but my absent mind, which their absence signifies.

And to love is not merely to desire something of the beloved; it is to desire the beloved entire. Even with so trivial a matter as the writer's love of lobster, there is something vaguely sinister about my desire to *possess* the lobster, to eat up the whole beast. This sinister shadow in fact shades our more exalted loves also: the love that eats up the beloved is all too well known, and fear of being thus devoured is surely some part of late modernity's famous "fear of commitment."

It may be already apparent where the hurt lies: the will to give and the will to possess make mischief at their intersection. This is so plainly the case that one of the most influential books[2] of twentieth-century theology proposed to cure many theological ills by separating gift and possession altogether, asserting that ἀγάπη and ἔρωσ, "love" as gift and "love" as desire, are simply two different things, and that one is what the real God does and his followers should do, and the other is what false gods and sinners and righteous pagans do. At first glance there do indeed seem to be instances where love is only the one or the other: the one who loves lobster desires to possess it, but does not apparently give himself to the beast; and one may devote oneself to, say, an institution, without apparently desiring to possess it.

It would doubtless solve some of our problem, if we could in this fashion simply distinguish desire and gift as two separate acts, and then set out to eschew the one and cultivate the other. But Nygren's contention has not held up well. Even the cases of lobster and institutional devotion do not perhaps sustain a more persistent reflection: someone who *really* loves lobster may in fact be said to "give himself to his meal"; and colleagues of someone deeply devoted to an institution may well suspect him or her of desire to take the place over.

Whether in our relation to God or to one another, gift and desire are, I think, not easily separable. Indeed, I think it is theologically dubious even to say that *God* loves with a purely disinterested ἀγάπη; he may not need us, but does he not *want* us? Moreover, if he loves us as sisters and brothers of the Son, do not, by the orthodox doctrine, the Father and the Son need each other? Precisely to be Father or Son? So that if it is once established that we are inalienable sisters and brothers of the Son, must not the Father indeed need us too? Is not God's love in fact ἔρωσ also? Jonathan Edwards regarded it as the

2. Anders Nygren, *Agape and Eros,* trans. A. G. Herbert (London, 1932). There have been three more English translations!

very fact of salvation, that because the Son is incarnate God is capable of desire for us.

Nietzsche's French epigones, apparently endorsing the analysis just now made, and claiming to experience with new intensity the dialectics of desire and love, have decided that love simply *is* death. I have nothing to give to my beloved but myself. But how am I to give *that?* So long as I have anything of myself left, I have not given all. But to have nothing of myself is to be dead — as, by no means by the by, all the mystics have said. How am I to give myself? Ultimately, the French Nietzscheans take their answer from Paul: "Greater love has no one. . . ." Christ's gift of himself is achieved by his death, and we are to die with him. But Paul knew of God who raises from the dead. Leave this God out, and indeed to love is simply to die and to call to die.[3]

II

The underlying situation is classically described in what is perhaps the most widely known and historically fateful passage in all the laborious works of Hegel: the passage on "Lordship and Slavery" from the *Phenomenology of Spirit.*[4] In this passage, Hegel sets up the situation that was later to be popularized as "I and Thou":[5] here are the two of us, face to face, addressing and responding to each other. It is the situation in which love must happen if it is to happen at all.

Hegel begins with the obvious: that as we address and respond to one another I am a subject and you are a subject. That is, I am knowing and addressing and willing you; and you are knowing and addressing and willing me. Then for me as subject you must be an object, that is, something known and willed and addressed, and for you as subject I must again be such an object.

3. To the intricate relation of postmodernism and love of death, see now John Milbank, *Theology and Social Theory* (Oxford: Blackwell, 1990), pp. 276-325.

4. *Phänomenologie des Geistes* (B.).iv.A.

5. Thousands of students suppose Martin Buber initiated the analysis.

But just so, the situation as Hegel describes it is the very impossibility of love. If you are my object while I abide in my subjectivity, you are my slave; to be an object of another who does the knowing and willing and addressing is what is meant by slavery. And of course vice versa. Thus the situation described by Hegel, in which each of us makes an object of the other, is one in which you and I try each to enslave the other, must each seek — to use the current jargon — hegemony. We could transcend this, in Hegel's diagnosis and in obvious fact, only if you were not *simply* my object, only if I allowed myself to be your object and you allowed yourself to be mine, if I allowed myself to be your slave and you did the same. By these abnegations each of us would be allowed to remain also a subject for the other, so as not in fact to be a slave; *mutually allowed* objectification would be no slavery.

The big question, however, and the postmodern question, is: How are we ever to accomplish this? The great motto of *Moulin Rouge* is, "All you need is to love and be loved in return." Indeed, but how are we to bring that off? In the movie, it is achieved by tuberculosis.

Hegel himself is finally no help. The *Phenomenology of Spirit* is the narrative of Spirit's *self*-quest and *self*-realization, which plays itself out in the self-quest and self-realization of each finite spirit, that is, each of us. The only escape from the mutual quest for domination, available for Hegel to commend, is that each of us act to eschew it — precisely in course of a personal quest for self-realization.

The passage on Lordship and Slavery is at once a true revelation of the human condition, and a bad pietistic sermon: "Let yourself be an object for your Thou. Eschew the lust for domination." The problem is the same as with most pietist sermons. "Only believe," the preacher winds up; which is all very well, but how do I do this, if I do not believe already? With Hegel's sermon: How do I let you make me your object, if I am not already and otherwise liberated from the subject-object impasse? How do I know you will reciprocate? Indeed, how am I not to think you certainly will not?

The great contribution of postmodernism is to have pondered

the situation as Hegel describes it, and under the tutelage of the twentieth century's horror drawn the obvious but earlier evaded conclusion, that indeed we *cannot* simply decide to stop enslaving each other, that "the other" I meet must always be the other whose otherness I posit for *my* own sake and so not a real other at all. If the way to transcend my will to dominate you, is to convert *myself* from that will, it will not happen, for of course the supposed conversion must itself be an act of that same will.[6] If we accept Hegel's account of the situation as I and Thou face each other, his exhortation must only add frustration to our mutual resentments, and our discourse must always remain a struggle to dominate. "Hell," said Sartre, a notably frustrated Hegelian, "is other people," and that not in the mass of third parties, but in the face-to-face where love would occur if it could occur at all.

So there we are, I and Thou, in the situation where we are called to love one another, and that very situation appears to make this impossible, locking us into struggle for domination, into desire without gift. Love, which is both, would appear to be impossible.

Of course, we certainly do sometimes seem nevertheless to love each other, but the "hermeneutics of suspicion" are there to disillusion us. I may think I love you and even act like I love you, but Freud or Nietzsche or Marx will be at hand to explain how this is a mere disguise for self-aggrandizement in one mode or another. Indeed — and this is a bit to the side — what the famous and praised hermeneutics of suspicion are at bottom suspicious of, is always and only love.[7]

Is there an escape? Two are on offer, that I know of.

I cannot, as myself, convert myself to accept my status as your object and so to accept you as a subject like me. But perhaps I can *abolish* myself, that is, abolish the difference between I and Thou. Perhaps you and I can avoid dominating each other by *becoming* each other, by abolishing our separate selfhoods.

6. Augustine's analyses, earlier reported, are decisive again here!

7. Even further to the side, that is why they are a hopeless way to approach the Scriptures, which are about love. A hermeneutics based on denial that the to-be-interpreted matter exists will devour itself.

This is, at any rate, a different project than self-conversion, and may even be possible, if just barely. Much of humanity has in fact seen it as the only possibility and set out to achieve it, usually by long and arduous training, by discipline so hard that in some concepts it can succeed only over millennia of rebirths. Since success would mean the also retrojective non-being of the trainee, it is hard to know if the project ever in fact succeeds. But I see no reason why it should not. The question is, Should we *want* to disappear into each other, should we want it to become true that "Thou art that," if love is our hope? The word "love" can stretch very far, but can it stretch to the situation where there are no longer separately identifiable someones to love and be loved?[8]

We should, anyway, be aware that much called "love" in modernity's decadence is in fact flight from personhood, the search for absorption into the other and of the other into me. The sixties' stage of the sexual revolution, with its group sex under drugs and similar assisted suicides of personal identity, shows this blatantly. That sort of "love, love, love" is no longer quite so prevalent, but only, I think, because its motivations and attitudes have been taken into the wider culture.

Alternatively, there is the postmodernist offer. This is simply to leave off trying to exercise agape-love. Love is eros, period. There is no escape from egocentrism and violence; every address, and most especially "I love you," is in fact an exercise of the will to power. That is the truth — and why should we not — as Nietzsche himself was wont to put it — *celebrate* this truth? Why not be *joyfully* self-assertive, and realize that this *is* love, the only love possible to finite beings? To do so, we need only interpret love unabashedly as desire, and experience desire as a natural force which I do not choose but which in the nobility of the strong simply flows through me. So I love lobster and you *exactly* in the same way, and that is an end of it. And if you love me, that is, if you want to devour me, then we will fight and one of us

8. Buddhism's recourse to boddhisatvas, who redemptively love and are loved precisely because they give up final enlightenment, is instructive.

will prove stronger and the other weaker, and we will delight in the conflict until one of us triumphs, and then so much the worse for the weaker. Hurrah for desire unmixed with either pity or *ressentiment,* the love of the superman!

Well — why not? Perhaps one might be given pause by the experience of the just finished century, the century for which Nietzsche prophesied superman's arrival. But no doubt our capacity to think that *we* are different would be up to that challenge as well.[9]

We have been exploring the seeming identity of love and death. There I and Thou are, called to love one another. I want to give myself to you, but how do I do that? How do I convert myself from my own subjectivity and its objectifying of everything else? Other than by dying? But then I am no longer there for you. I want to possess you, but how do I do even that? Other than by devouring you? But then you are no longer there for me — the problem with the joy of eating a lobster is that eventually you have done it. And the ways on offer of breaking the Hegelian bypass only reinforce the identity of love and death, and thereby the seeming final impossibility of love.

III

It is time to stand back from these cogitations and recognize two facts, which will guide all that is to follow. One is the fact that according to the gospel people can and do succeed in loving, that the hermeneutics of suspicion are simply wrong. And the other is the fact of the triune God.

The philosophers' "I and Thou" can never love each other; let us take that as given. But you and I as actual persons nevertheless sometimes do. We do it, I suggest, when the famous I-Thou situation is transcended, not by some emergent from our pairing, but by something much simpler, by a third party who is outside the pairing and

9. We seem easily able to persuade ourselves that our eugenics by mass execution are of course nothing like the Nazis' eugenics by mass execution.

its indeed inevitable struggle. What can and sometimes does break you and me out of the mutual struggle for hegemony is someone who objectivizes both of us, in a particular way: who intends us to be lovers of each other.

Also Hegel and the French know, of course, that there are third parties around, and that you and I may take account of them in our confrontation, and even that this may sometimes a little ameliorate the struggle. But that is not the point vital to be made. The third party I here invoke is not a bystander, or even someone of whom *we* must take account in our face-off; this third party appears as an *agent* of our I-Thou relation, he or she appears as a subject who makes both you and me his or her objects, and whose intention for us as objects is precisely that we love each other.

This actually happens, incessantly. The presence — or even lamented absence — of the child, who wills the parents to love each other, enables the perdurance of marriage. This is the reason sexual love indeed begins as desire and must be turned into eros *and* agape by familial life. It is, moreover, much of the connection between sexual love and procreation, so regularly overlooked in contemporary chatter. On a tangent line, when mutual sexual exploitation is to become love, a judge or minister dictates and oversees a contract — and when that contract was enforceable, there was much more love around. Less decisively and at random: when economic or national parties are at genuine odds, when they are not already reconciled, mediators are needed; when acquaintance was seriously thought of as an opportunity of friendship, introductions were an essential part of social existence; when my friend and I begin to shout, we need one of our spouses to change the subject.

Without the third party, either desire undoes gift, and so turns love into struggle; or the dream of pure giving turns love into a quest for nothingness. Either way, the equation of love with death appears. To be sure, the third party who intends us to love each other, and rescues us from the I-Thou standoff, has him or herself an interest in our love; and between him or her and either of us this will generate the whole problematic again, but that is external to our relation to each other.

A fresh antinomy does, however, appear just at this point. The third party who intends you and me to love each other is in that intention a Thou for each of you and me, and between the third party and you, and between the third party and me, all the dismal dialectics just traced will therefore recur. How can it be that he or she truly wants me to love you? For surely this intention is itself an act of love for me? And so impossible in its turn?

IV

Plainly, what is needed is a third party who does not fall into the same situation with you or with me, that we are in with each other. Christian theology proposes the reality of such a third party, the Holy Spirit.

In this matter as in those taken up in previous chapters, the needed insight is: to solve our problem about the possibility of love, we need to look not to ourselves, but to God, and indeed to the actual God, the triune God. To put it as schematically as possible, the triune God is in himself a paired I and Thou with a Third Party, who because they are infinite do not have our problem.

In classical trinitarian theology, the Father and the Son are in exactly the situation described by Hegel — indeed, that is the ultimate source of Hegel's vision of I and Thou. In the standard trinitarian language: the Father begets the Son and the Son is begotten by the Father, and they are to love each other. Again, the Father speaks his Word, and the Word that is spoken is so perfect an expression of the Father that like the Father he is a speaker, so that each addresses the other as a subject and thereby objectifies the other — and there we are with the *Phenomenology of Spirit.*

Now — why are not the Father and God the Son locked in mutual struggle for domination? Within Christian theology the question supposes a possibility contrary not merely to fact but to possibility itself, but the question itself is far from absurd; the religions of the world generally posit precisely such a problematic at the heart of deity. Within Christian theology the question can therefore be posed as a thought-experiment.

The standard pattern of religion is always polytheistic. Necessarily, polytheistic religions tell stories of the relations between the gods, since were the gods not related to each other the universe they govern would be as chaotically pointless with them as without them. And at the heart of the stories there is always death between some pre-potent I and Thou: a sibling kills a sibling, or a child kills a parent, or a husband kills a wife. Thus the central myth of classical Greek religion, which gives meaning to the Greeks' universe, is Father Time's slaying of his sons, until the one son Zeus slays him.

Where simple polytheism is overcome, the replacement is one or another doctrine of emanation. From a first principle a second principle proceeds, and then perhaps a third and so on until the processions reach the empirical world to be interpreted. The problem at the heart of every such vision is the inability of the first principle to let go; in the language of trinitarianism, of the Father to let go of the Son. What emanates from the first principle either never becomes truly *other* than it, or is finally illusion, or if truly other and real is just so evil. For a familiar modern version of this mythology one may think of Freud's mythology of the Oedipal complex.

If I may put it so: what rescues the real God the Father and the real God the Son from the Hegelian face-off, from Oedipal mutual bondage, is God the Spirit, whose biblical role is precisely that he is freedom and love. The Spirit intends the Father and the Son, and the Spirit's intention for them is that they shall love one another. The Spirit frees the Father to let the Son go, and so actually to love him. The Spirit frees the Son from servility to the Father, and so actually to love him.

Why then do not the Father and the Spirit with each other, or the Son and the Spirit with each other, fall into the Hegelian trap, as a created third party does with you and with me? The Spirit is both the one who intends the Father and the Son to love one another *and* in classical doctrine is himself the love between them: within God the Spirit exhausts himself in the gift he gives — here is the moment of truth in Eastern doctrines of self-emptying. After all, spirit is always *someone's* spirit and nothing else; the Holy Spirit is the Spirit *of* the Father and the Son whom the Spirit lets love one another, and he is nothing else at all. Or we may say: Father, Son, and Spirit are, precisely in the utter mutuality which the Spirit enables and is, but one and the same only God, so that there is and can be no conflict between them. Which is precisely the difference between God and us.

V

But what has all this to do with *our* problem? Just this: the Spirit who frees the Father and the Son to love each other, and who thereupon is their love, is the very Spirit who animates the church. In the church, every human third party is animated by that very Spirit who does not fall into mutual bondage with those whom he frees to love one another.

I do not mean this in any spiritualist fashion; my assertions are about daily life in the church. The third human party who in the church reconciles me and my fellow believer does not do so in his or her own name, but in the name "of the Father, and of the Son, and of the Spirit." With my pastor I may very well be on the outs, but the Spirit in whose power the pastor speaks, has another relation to me altogether, internal to the relation he has to Jesus the Son. The eucharistic president who binds me and the one next me into, as Paul says, one Spirit, by giving us one cup and one bread, to make us, as again Paul says, one body, may simultaneously be involved in some church-political brawl with both of us, but that cannot impede the Spirit.

We have to be as arrogant as the New Testament is. Love is the *new* commandment given to a new kind of community, the church; that we "little children" should "love one another," is not so much a command as a reminder of what we are in this unprecedented society. The church is the home of love in this world.

Does this mean that there is no love outside the church? No, for this Spirit is the Creator-Spirit. Wherever there is spontaneity in creation, even in natural process, what is happening is in fact the freedom that the Spirit is. And wherever there is freedom, Hegel's face-off is broken and love can happen. So love is both a new commandment and the original energy of all things. If only we are not intimidated by the hermeneuts of suspicion, we will see it: love is indeed what makes the world turn. It is an insight much needed by both church and world: contrary to nearly all late-modern or postmodern doctrine, including some Christian theological proposals, love is not uncommon. Hatred and death are of course all around. But so is love.

Were we left where Hegel left us, where the only spirit is the one realizing it*self* through us, where for us to love each other I have somehow for my own sake to perform the good work of letting you make me your object, we would remain in the situation of which Nietzsche saw the terrible secret. But we are not left in this situation. There is the triune God, and he can be love, and he can take us into his love.

We need not hurt the one we love. Indeed we will not. For there is the Spirit.